Contents

Acknowledgements

Preface

Introduction   **1**

There's no one quite like Grammar   **5**

Punctuation   **15**

Is it clear?   **27**

Away with words   **33**

Padding   **39**

Everyday words   **51**

Shortening sentences   **61**

Jargon and social services speak   **71**

Gobbledygook   **83**

Being human   **87**

A matter of style   **95**

Good by design   **107**

Dos, don'ts and maybes   **115**

Putting it all together   **121**

Conclusion   **127**

Sources   **131**

Index   **133**

Acknowledgements

I'm sure no book can ever be just the work of one person. This one certainly wasn't. With so many people to thank it's a task and a half to try to make it sound as unlike an Oscar acceptance speech as possible. Still here goes...

I'd like to thank Kathryn Stone, a good friend, mentor and agent who really is responsible for this book happening - so, if you hate it, blame her; all those people who waded through the early drafts, who came up with suggestions that make me look like a better writer than I probably am, who feared little for our friendships by telling me which bits were rubbish, and who gleefully highlighted all my tpying erorrs (thanks) - Eric Davis (sky blue army doctor); Marcus Woolley (Conan the Librarian), Frances Rostron (in distant solidarity); Edward Kenny (top man); Julie Cann (and does); Kes ('you *can't* say that'); *and* special thanks to Jo Hopkins ('I heard that, you'). Also to my brother Ian Hopkins for laughing (mostly at the bits he was meant to). Many thanks to you all. Thanks also to Geoffrey Mann and Martin Jones at Russell House for support, advice and for taking the chance. A sound move to thank the publishers, methinks.

And finally, thanks to Stephen Hicks for illustrating the book.

Graham Hopkins

Plain
English
for
Social
Services

Graham Hopkins

Russell House Publishing

Dedication

For my mum, Edith Maud Hopkins
I love and miss you

First published in 1998 by

Russell House Publishing Limited
4 St. George's House
Uplyme Road Business Park
Lyme Regis
Dorset
DT7 3LS

© Graham Hopkins

British Library Cataloguing-in-Publication Data:
A catalogue record for this book is available from the British Library.

ISBN: 1-898924-14-7

Printed by Short Run Press, Exeter
Typeset by Interleaf Productions Limited, Sheffield

Preface

Plain English for Social Services is for those people in social care and other related services who write for the public.

The purpose of the book is to introduce and promote the principles of plain English - but to do so in a deliberately informal and readable way. It draws on examples made public in 26 social services departments in England and Wales and six social work departments in Scotland.

Plain English for Social Services will enable you to improve **how** you write. Its companion volume, *The Write Stuff*, gives advice on improving the quality of **what** you write and will help you get your message across.

The Write Stuff is a good practice guide, for people working in social care and related fields, that shows you how to plan, research, structure, write and edit your written work. Drawing on practical examples, it will help you to write letters, memos, reports and court submissions, or simply fill in or produce a standard letter or form.

Writing is a skill, not just something we should be expected to know how to do. *Plain English* and *The Write Stuff* will help you to do it better.

Chapter 1

Introduction

Introduction

Fulfilment: it is the policy of the borough to recognise that fulfilment is the function of personal desires and the utilization of possessed abilities in all that daily life offers; the art of gainful employment of mind and body.

I wrote that. It was October 1993 and I probably wasn't feeling very well at the time. It was how I defined 'fulfilment', one of the so-called six principles of care. The other five principles - privacy, dignity, choice, independence and rights - were at least as pompous. I later realised the error of my words. Nobody understood them. I wasn't mindful of my audience. If anything, I was mindempty of them.

I realised that I was writing to **impress** and not writing to **inform**.

I don't just try and dismiss it with all that 'the past is a foreign country' thing, either. It travels further than that. Indeed, just as the ex-smoker can be the least tolerant of smoking, so now I lack all tolerance for pompous-filled phrases and jargon-filled pages.

Writing for social services is not about displaying a wide vocabulary or writing in wine and roses. Nor is it about wrapping your meaning in your best 'look at me' words. It's about communicating with people. It's about helping people understand. It may not be rocket science, but it's not easy.

This book is for those people in social care and other related services who write for the public. The purpose of the book is to introduce and promote the principles of plain English but to do so in a deliberately informal and readable way. It draws on examples made public by 29 social services departments in England and Wales and six social work departments in Scotland. However, in the best of social work traditions, it treats all examples in confidence. All names and dates are made up and any identifying material has been edited.

If, having read the book you have been entertainingly informed, I'll be happy. Or at least more cheerful than I was when one of my colleagues, knowing that I was writing this book, dug up one of my old inspection reports. At that time the working title for the book was *'So, what you're saying is...'* before unbridled wit gave our book its final resting name. My colleague, bless her little cotton socks, had helpfully written across the expertly photocopied excerpt: 'So, what you're saying is ... what exactly?' The offending item was:

> *'There is a variety of chairs and individual choice in colour and size of napkins which is encouraged. This helps negate uniformity, espouses individuality and is commended'.*

Quite simply, I have to hold up my hand and say that this was poor writing. It failed in its purpose. In *The Good English Guide*, Godfrey Howard recognises that plain English should not guide all writing. But it does have its place. And it is there, in those areas where it is our duty to inform that plain English should be at the heart of what we write. *'In that world,'* Howard says, *'if we make others struggle to understand what we are writing or saying, we are using bad English, rotten to the core'.*

If you are going to write something well, there are three basic questions you need to answer: why are you writing it? - *the objective*; what do you want to happen as a result of it? - *the outcome*; and who are you writing it for? - *the target audience*. The first two cannot be achieved without understanding the importance of the last one.

A social work student could confidently write the following without batting an ink well. *'The use of proxemics attempted to prevent a power differential in which myself as practitioner could possibly convey messages of oppression and authoritarianism'.* As part of their portfolio it would, no doubt, be worth a few marks. But it will only be read by a couple of lecturers in social work. Or three if it goes to an external assessor - as the highest marked paper, I shouldn't wonder. It is writing that is fit for its purpose. However, take that sentence out of the campus and it is meaningless. You could argue that writing for academic success is like taking a driving test: you do what they want you to do and then, once you've passed, you've got to teach yourself how to drive in the real world. This book is here to help you to teach yourself how to write in the real world.

The following quote from a leaflet might seem okay on first reading. There's some light jargon but most people who work in social services should understand it.

> *'The current programme overleaf, offers a choice of work and skills training in the small group work principle. Our aim is to help you enhance your social skills sufficiently in order to enable you to take an active part in your personal development'.*

However, this was handed out to clients at a day service for people with learning disabilities. It might as well be written in Old Norse.

It's all about your target audience. A memo to a colleague can be brimming with jargon (it can be a useful shorthand after all) because the likelihood is that it will be understood. However, I do believe that even when communicating with others in social care, we could all come back to earth a bit. We could all do with becoming a bit more human.

While reading this book, if you:

- smile
- laugh out loud
- shake your head slowly while tut-tutting
- squirm uncomfortably in your seat
- think 'my manager needs to read this'

then I guess I will have done my job.

But if you go back to your place of work and dig out every standard letter to see if it's clear, understandable and user-friendly; or start thinking 'will *everyone* understand this?' *every* time you write something; then, and only then, will I *know* that I have done my job. Go to it.

Chapter 2

There's no one quite like Grammar

There's no one quite like Grammar

'An intelligent child who is bidden to spell debt and very properly spells it d-e-t, is caned for not spelling it with a 'b' because Julius Caesar spelt it with a 'b''.

- George Bernard Shaw

Grammar can be fun.

Yes, I've actually read this. Unbelievable, I know. I bet they think that sticking pins in their eyes is a hoot, too. English grammar is a strange beast. Hardly any ordinary citizen has anything other than a basic grasp of its workings. And yet some people will defend their limited understanding of grammar up to the point of pistols at dawn.

Being a disrespectful sort at the best of times, I've argued against such things as split infinitives (usually getting onto the subject by way of Star Trek recollections) with people who react as if I've just confessed to adultery with their partners, introduced their children to illegal chemicals and burnt their house down. Which, of course, I only intended to do a week later.

There's a popular misconception that English grammar is made up of rules and regulations that must be obeyed at all times or else you will be guilty of social inadequacy. It isn't. Or rather it is and it isn't. Quite often grammar is nothing more than a series of differing attitudes and opinions. Some things clearly are indisputable. A sentence starts with a capital letter and window is spelt w-i-n-d-o-w. But whether *council* starts with a capital letter or not is more a matter of style than regulation.

But fear not, I don't intend to come over all scholarly or knowledgeable on the subject. Grammar is an immense subject, almost as huge as the disdain I have for it. And life is too short and my palette too fussy to chew both over. Disdain is simply more to my taste. The intricacies, delicacies and complexities of grammar are best left out of a book like this. If you're a dedicated follower of pedantry, with a wealth of linguistics to spend, go shop elsewhere. This is the bargain basement. And on the final day of the biggest sale ever.

Most people wouldn't know a *dangling participle* if it walked up to them and slapped their face. The only way I could explain what *a modal auxiliary verb* is, or, come to that, a *non-defining relative clause* or a *verb of incomplete predication* or a *double genitive* (with tonic, no doubt) would be to look them up. And I'd really rather not, if it's all the same to you.

The Latin connection

Grammar's never going to produce a *Now That's What I Call Grammar 26* to soar up the nation's popular culture hit parade. One problem with English grammar is the undue and overbearing influence of Ancient Greek and, mainly, Latin. Up until the 19th century these two languages were thought to be the only languages worthy of study. Those who set about bringing order to the English language, following the invention of the printing press, have for centuries looked to Latin for guidance. So the rules of a dead language have been applied to a live and dynamic language. In *Mother Tongue*, Bill Bryson wrote that '*making English grammar conform to Latin rules is like asking people to play baseball using the rules of football. It's a patent absurdity*'.

Godfrey Howard in *The Good English Guide*, wrote that while there are still those who cling to the traditional prescriptive grammar based on Latin, the '*more enlightened view now is that the fossilized laws of a dead language are a meaningless straitjacket to impose on English*'.

Prescriptive and descriptive

The two opposing camps are the prescriptive grammarians and the descriptive grammarians. The *prescriptive* camp declare an undying oath of loyalty to deciding what should be used and how it should be used in English. Whereas the *descriptive* camp seek to '*describe how it is used objectively, accurately, systematically, and comprehensively*'. (The Oxford Companion to the English Language).

The prescriptive camp view the French language, or rather they view the Académie Française, with an envious eye. The Académie has complete control of the language. It decides what is right and whether new words are to be accepted or not. It defines and defends the language. Ever since the reign of Charles II (1660-1685) patrons and scholars have tried to set up an academy to define English once and for all. They've failed every time. One of the more recent was the BBC Advisory Committee on Spoken English. The Committee sought to bring authority and regulation to 'Received Pronunciation' (or *BBC English* or *The Queen's English* or *lah-di-dah* depending on your perspective). It was set up in 1926. On its demise, the then Director-General of the BBC, Lord Reith concluded that the English language has '*no experts - only users*'.

Indeed users have great influence over English. It is a most democratic language. Words like organization (the 'correct' English spelling) is now recognised by all dictionaries to be organisation (the popular spelling). It does seem fruitless to do otherwise. Similarly, words end up with new or different meanings because of popular misunderstanding. For example, *disinterested* which means *impartial* is commonly used to mean *uninterested*. Also, people regularly advise others when they are not actually giving advice about anything but are rather *informing* them of something.

But does it sound right?

For many of us, English is like most things in our lives, we just get on with it. And yet despite all its complexities we often know instinctively whether something sounds right or not. Indeed, that is the odd beauty of English grammar. *The Oxford Guide to English Usage* provides plain advice that comes with tons more authority than I could ever hope to muster: '*One should be guided by what sounds right*'. Hear, hear.

The years of Tory rule from 1979 to 1997 may have, in part, been characterised by riots, unemployment and increasing crime. But, the then prime minister, John Major knew why. He had his finger on the pulse. He knew that it all had nothing to do with deprivation, poverty, social dissatisfaction or anything like that. Oh no, he felt that all the country's problems could be solved by a return to teaching basic grammar. If people understood a dangling modifier then, hey presto, everything would be rosy in England's green and pleasant. However, a return to formal grammar teaching is thankfully unlikely. The National Union of Teachers declared that any such return would '*run counter to everything which is known about language development*'.

So, it looks as if it really is goodbye, Mr Chips.

▌ Short guide to grammatical terms

abstract and concrete

Sir Ernest Gowers in *The Complete Plain Words* advises against what he calls '*the lure of the abstract*' by saying that the '*reason for preferring the concrete to the abstract is clear. Your purpose must be to make your meaning plain*'. Concrete words are precise words that leave the reader in no doubt what is meant. *Colour, outdoor play area* and *vehicle* are abstract words but *sky blue, garden* and *car* are concrete. For example, in social services, *establishment* would be an abstract word and *home* a concrete word. You should look to be specific rather than vague. For example, prefer *The leaflet will be translated into Turkish* rather than *The leaflet will be translated into a community language*.

adjectives

Adjectives are descriptive words. They describe a noun (a *good* social worker, an *effective* department, an *interesting* article). I'm not sure why we still say *adjectives* when *descriptive words* does the job so much better. How often do we hear that an '*adjective is a descriptive word*'? If we keep having to explain what an adjective is with a more easily understood phrase, why not just use the more easily understood phrase?

adverbs

Professional grammarians divide adverbs into four groups: adjuncts, subjuncts, disjuncts and conjuncts. Luckily, we don't need to worry about that. All we need to know is that an adverb generally ends in -ly and adds something to the verb. It tell us something about it (*They responded promptly* - the adverb *promptly* tell us about the verb *responded*). There is another kind of adverb that tell us to what extent an adjective is being used (*The training course was **rather** dull*). And, rather confusingly, adverbs can also tell us to what extent other adverbs are used (*They responded **very** promptly*).

clause

From the Latin *clausa*, meaning 'the close of a sentence'. A clause is a complete series of words that seem like a sentence within a sentence. An example would be *because he was told to* in: 'He wrote jargon because he was told to'. A clause can also be a sentence if the sentence is simple, in that it has only one piece of information: 'He wrote a lot of jargon'.

conjunctions

A Latinate word that means 'joining together'. Words like *and, or, but, because, if, although* are conjunctions. Grammarians gnash their teeth at the thought of using conjunctions at the start of sentences. But fear not, you can argue that they join sentences together. And that's that.

contraction

Contractions are words that have been shortened by leaving out letters and replacing them with an apostrophe. So *cannot* as a contraction is *can't*, will not = won't, didn't = did not, hasn't = has not, isn't = is not, and so on. There is a belief that contractions are too informal for official writing. This depends entirely on the purpose of your writing. There is no doubt that (most) contractions can read better than their in-full counterparts and bring some warmth to your writing. If the purpose of your writing is to inform, explain or encourage then contractions are valid. This book makes full use of them - although not in this section. If you feel more formality is required (a written warning to a member of staff, a letter threatening the cancellation of a childminder's registration, an eviction notice) then do not use them.

definite article

The technical term for *the*.

direct and indirect speech

Direct speech puts the words actually used by someone into speech marks (or inverted commas or quotation marks or quotes): *'This is the best nursery in town,' said a parent.* Indirect speech describes what has been said rather than directly quoting: *One parent said this was the best nursery in town.* Whether you use double speech marks ["..."] or single ones ['...'] is largely a matter of style. It seems in the 90s we're happier with the single set.

indefinite article

The technical term for *a* and *an*.

infinitive

An infinitive is *to* followed by a verb: *to review, to assess, to acknowledge.* In Latin present tense infinitives are one word and can't be split. An infinitive is split when a word comes between the to and the verb: to *regularly* review, to *completely* assess, to *fully* acknowledge. To do this is to drive the ravens from the Tower of London. Or rather it is to *immediately* drive the ravens from the Tower. The most famous split infinitive belongs to Star Trek: *'to boldly go'* rather than *'to go boldly'*. So, to split or not to split? There's nothing to worry about here. Let your ear be your guide. If your phrase has a better rhythm with a split infinitive, then split it. *To fully appreciate the situation* sounds better than *to appreciate fully the situation.* A better writer than any of us writing in the personal social services deserves the final word on the matter. Raymond Chandler when told that he made some 'mistakes' in a transcript, told the hapless editor that *'when I split an infinitive, godammit, it stays split'*.

nouns

Nouns name a creature, thing or idea. Nouns are divided into four groups. *Common nouns* name classes of people or things: woman, language, book, service users, council.

Proper nouns name one special or individual person or thing and are usually spelt with a capital letter as they are names of people, places and so on: Edward Kenny, Barking and Dagenham Council, Ford's.

Collective nouns name groups of people, animals or things: committee of councillors, pack of cards. The difficulty with collective names of people is whether to treat them as singular or plural. For example, should it be *the Advisory Group has* or *the Advisory Group have*? It's all to do with perception: do you see the group as a whole (singular) or something made up of a number of individual people (plural). I prefer the plural. It also sounds better to say *the council have* rather than *the council has*. It somehow sounds warmer and less abrupt. You're seeing it as people rather than as a thing. But be consistent. You should say *the council **have** decided **their** policy* or *the council **has** decided **its** policy*.

Abstract nouns name qualities, actions, feelings and so on: idealism, patience, honesty, health, temptation.

prepositions

Prepositions are usually small words (*like, in, on, to, from, into, over, before*) used to show how other words in a phrase or sentence relate to each other. For example: the manager went *into* the office; the clients came *from* the day centre; the rooms differed *in* style. Preposition is based on Greek and Latin words meaning *putting before*. This is why grammarians will tell you (if you're unlucky enough to be cornered by one) that prepositions simply can't be put at the end of sentences, because how can it be before something if it's at the end? Most prepositions *are* put before words but there are times when it is sensible to have them at the end. For example: what did you do that for?; which home are you living in?; the centre's nothing to look at. There will still be people who will prefer 'into which file did you put it?' rather than 'which file did you put it in?'. But you should let your ear guide you. If a preposition sounds better at the end, leave it there.

pronouns

Pronouns are words used instead of nouns to save the clumsiness of having to keep repeating them. So, instead of *The manager read the manager's report and then put it in the manger's file*, you can write *The manager read **her** report and then put it in **her** file*. However, make sure it's clear what pronoun is relating to which noun. Unlike the following example, where it's not clear who's put whose jumper on whose chair: *The key worker spoke to her client and she said she would agree to her putting her jumper on her chair.*

tenses

The form of the verb which indicates when the action took place is called its tense. If it's yet to happen it's called the future tense. If it's happening now, it's called the present tense. If it's already happened, it's called the past tense. There are some variations on the theme (the non-progressive perfect, the past continuous) but stick to the theme.

Some people get hung up on trying not to mix up their tenses. But sometimes it is inevitable. An inspection report written completely in the past tense is fine on the whole as it's reporting on what happened during an inspection that took place sometime before. However, to write that *'the home was in a residential area'* is a touch absurd. Unless, of course, the home has moved since the inspection. Or, indeed woke up one morning and found that the residential area had done a bunk.

verbs

Verbs are the part of speech that express action. A verb is a *doing* word. A verb has tense and tells you whether something is happening, is about to happen or has happened. So a client may have already walked to the shops, is about to walk to them or is walking that way as we speak.

Chapter 3

Punctuation

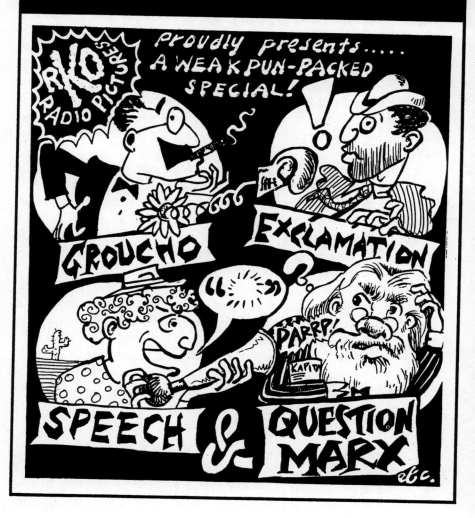

Punctuation

2, 4; 6: 8? Punctuate!

I'm not sure why but some people view punctuation with the relish of a social worker writing logs up or doing duty on a Friday afternoon. It has no right to create the fear it does. It has one simple task - to make written language easier to read. That's *why* we punctuate. *How* we punctuate is significantly a matter of style. It may be a style adopted parrot-fashion from your English teacher. Or it may be your council, department or manager's style. Or it may be your own quaint, cute, curious, bold, brash or in-your-face style. But it is the stuff of style, nonetheless.

It's been said that words in sentences are like parts of a machine. If you don't need them, don't use them. Taking this analogy one step further, punctuation is like the nuts and bolts that keep all the parts together. You should only use the punctuation you need. If a comma makes it easier to read a sentence then use it. If not, don't. If you use too little punctuation, your meaning might be lost or difficult to find. If you use too much, it looks unsightly and wastes your time.

In terms of plain English you should make more use of the full stop than the comma. The colon and semi-colon, if used at all, usually get their chance to shine when the writer makes a vertical list. People generally understand the distinctions between the roles of full stops and commas. You can't say the same for colons and semi-colons. However, this should not signal their demise. The subtleties may be lost on people but they'll understand that some kind of pause is expected and that's usually good enough for the writing we use.

Full stops [.]

A full stop signifies the end of a sentence. Short sentences help deliver information in manageable and comfortable bursts. This means that the full stop (or *stop* or *period*) should get more work than any other punctuation mark.

There's no need in these fast-living times to use full stops for abbreviations (Ms, Mr, St, BBC, USA) or initials (GP, MP). Even initials for names (E M Forster, W G Grace) aren't essential. The reason is that a full stop would signify a shortened word. But as people know that USA is short for *United States of America* we simply don't need to have U.S.A. to remind us. The same applies to numbers such as dates. We don't need to use the full stop when we write '*30th.*' anymore as '*30*th' will do (indeed '*30*' will do). You can even hold a demo on the first Tues in Jan, if you really had to. Acronyms, words spelt out by initials, such as DIAL (Disablement Information and Advice Line) have shed the stops also.

Commas [,]

In plain English terms commas are targets for potential full stops. Use them sparingly. But, nonetheless, they have an important role to play in making sense of what is written.

In days of yore we could spray commas all over the place. The first commas to go were those used on addresses. No more do we painstakingly scribe with our quill and feather:

Mr. W. G. Strachan, O.B.E.,	*Mr W G Strachan OBE*
King Richard St.,	*King Richard St*
Coventry,	*Coventry*
West Midlands.	*West Midlands*

We are in the days of punctuation-free addresses and dates (1 April 1998 not 1st., April, 1998). You no longer need the comma to follow your *Dear Mr Strachan* or your signing off *yours sincerely*.

Use commas to separate words on a list:
'*Regular health checks are carried out on the eyes, ears, teeth and feet*'.
You don't usually need to add a comma before the *and* at the end of list. But there are times when you will need to do so to make your meaning clear. The following example of this comes from a public spirited advert at a bus stop. It read:

> 'Lend a hand. Elderly people, disabled people, those
> carrying shopping and parents with small children might
> appreciate some assistance'.

You would think that those with shopping would have enough to carry
without having to carry parents with small children as well. Again a
comma prevents the double take:

> 'Lend a hand. Elderly people, disabled people, those
> carrying shopping, and parents with small children might
> appreciate some assistance'.

Similarly:

> 'Three Standards were examined - Privacy and Respect,
> Independence and Choice, and Fulfilment'.

Without the final comma we may well think that that the 'Privacy and
Respect' is one standard, 'Independence' a second, and 'Choice and
Fulfilment' a third.

Also, as in this example from the magazine **Community Care**:

> 'The work will be phased over the next five years to
> minimise disruption to residents, and staffing levels will
> be increased as the project is completed'.

As you can see, if the comma before *and* had been left out you might
assume that there would be minimum disruption to residents *and* staffing
levels.

Use commas to separate parts of a sentence:

> 'Although children are mainly white British, real efforts
> are being made to offer 'international' foods'.

Also, as in this example from **Community Care**:

> 'A Social Services Inspectorate report highlighted the fact
> that, in some areas, domestic violence is a factor in 20
> per cent of allocated social work cases, while a third of

children on child protection registers have mothers who
have been the targets of violence'.

Use commas to provide an information 'aside' in a sentence.

'Records show that the supervision structure in the
home, which was introduced in 1997, is working well'.

Commas used to surround certain phrases such as *in the meantime, as*
a matter of fact, and *of course.* And words like *nevertheless, perhaps,*
understandably and *however.*

'This, of course, means the review can now take place'.

'Staff, understandably, feel upset by this'.

However, this is not always necessary. If you feel it helps, then use them.
If not, don't.

Colons [:] and semi colons [;]

I asked some people if they knew what a colon was. My brother thought
it was a film role played by Arnold Schwarzenegger: Colon the Barbarian.
He came the closest. Somebody else mentioned something unfortunate
to do with irrigation and weight loss, which is best left to those moving
in Harley Street circles.

The colon stands for 'as follows'. It usually finds itself at the front of a
list of things or a quotation. If you are listing things, a comma is usually
enough to act as a separator.

'There were concerns picked up at the last review: budget
planning, shopping skills, interaction with strangers, and
menu planning'.

A colon can also be used in a more refined way when a statement either
explains or follows on from the one before: as in the following example
from *Community Care.*

'Women's Aid points to the severe shortage of refuges:
there are just 240 in the whole country'.

A semi-colon is really a halfway house between a comma and a full stop. If you create a vertical list starting with a colon, it is conventional (but not compulsory) to sub-divide each point with a semi-colon.

'The concerns picked up at the last review were:

- *understanding money;*
- *shopping skills;*
- *interaction with strangers; and*
- *menu planning'.*

However, this book's preferred style is to leave out punctuation on lists. Each listed item clearly stands out in its own right. To use semi-colons is merely a conventional add-on rather than serving any purpose of clarification. Be daring.

A semi-colon is also useful if the separation between the listed items needs to be more definite:

'Plain English has many parts: using everyday words, which means avoiding big words where possible; avoiding jargon, as people outside of the 'in crowd' cannot understand; shortening sentences, which helps people understand more easily what's being written; and so on...'

There is no need to put a dash after a colon [:-]. They are two different punctuation marks but in this sense are doing the same job. Choose one or t'other. To use both is pointless. Smash convention. Overthrow tradition. Destroy the status quo (well, they are getting on a bit). Prefer a dash-less colon.

Exclamation marks [!]

These show strong emotions such as surprise, anger or dismay. They usually follow exclamations (Agghh!). However, most people recognise them as big neon-lighted signposts for punchlines, witticisms and assorted jokes.

'The Director's popularity is on the increase. Last night someone touched him with a barge pole!'

To use them in this way is heavy handed. One exclamation mark can be three too many. So, if you really have to use one, make sure it is just the one. Resist the temptation to put loads of them at the end!!! If what you say is funny, people will laugh: exclamation mark or not.

Question marks [?]

If it's a question of you writing a question, then use one of these at the end of it. No question.

Apostrophes [']

The apostrophe causes plenty of pain, anguish and suffering. For those of you who suffer (and take heart for you are many) the advice you probably want to hear is - pretend they don't exist and deny all knowledge of them. But the rules are really quite simple.

Use the apostrophe to show possession.

If the noun is singular add apostrophe s.	**The social worker's report.** **The home's aims and objectives** **The review's findings.**
If the noun is plural ending in s, add just an apostrophe.	**Parents' comments (comments made by more than one parent)**
If the noun is plural, not ending in s, add apostrophe s.	**The children's toys.** **The women's group.**

Given that English is a language that changes with popular usage (or abusage), the apostrophe is duelling with a date in punctuation's Boot

Hill. Surely nothing is more misunderstood or misused in our language than the apostrophe. Typical mistakes include the following.

'There was a record of each staff members' next of kin'.

This refers to each member of staff, so staff member is a singular noun. The apostrophe goes before the *s* (**member's**).

'Client's views are sought on the service they provide'.

This clearly means more than one client. Or else it would have read 'A client's views were...'. The noun (clients) is plural so only the apostrophe is added to the *s* (**clients'**).

'Early assessments are seen as essential in promoting peoples well being'.

The noun *people* is plural. But as it does not end in *s*, you need to add apostrophe *s* (**people's**).

'Both resident's spoke of the kindness they had received'.

As no possession is implied, the word **residents** needs no apostrophe.

'The Children's Act 1989'.

It's remarkable how often people make this mistake. The correct title is the **Children Act 1989**. It's an act *about* children, not *owned by* them. In the same way, an apostrophe isn't needed for either Citizens Advice Bureau (an advice bureau *for* citizens, not owned by them) or Day Centre Staff Guidelines (guidelines *for* staff, not owned by them).

Possessive pronouns don't take apostrophes. Words such as *hers, theirs, its, ours* are already possessive. This is confusing to some. *The council's policy* is correct. However, if you replace *council* for the pronoun *it*, you would logically add apostrophe *s* - **it's** policy. Er, no. Logic is not the best guide when it comes to English. Because English has contractions (*can't* contract, *won't* contract) whenever you see *it's* it will always mean either *it is* or *it has*. So if you're ever confused whether it should be *its* or *it's*, read the sentence back to yourself replacing *it's* or *its* with *it is*. If it makes sense it's *it's* for you. If not, it's *its*. I think.

There has also been a tendency to use an apostrophe for the plural of abbreviations.

> *'There are a number of GP's who have worked in the borough since the early 1970's'.*

This is no longer necessary. We can now write about GPs and the 1970s and, come to that, Under 8s. However, some things such as letters still don't seem right without an apostrophe. Until that changes we'll have to continue to mind our p's and q's instead of ps and qs.

Hyphens [-]

'Hyphens are hell'. So said Phillip Howard, literary editor of The Times. There is little hope in our lifetime of achieving universal agreement about when hyphens should be used and when they shouldn't. But the best guide for using hyphens or not is: are they necessary? If by using a hyphen you make your potentially ambiguous statement clear, then use one. There's little need to write *a three-year-old child*. But *three year old children* could cause a problem: is it children who are three years old or three children who are a year old?

Also compound words (multi-cultural, inter-agency, self-administer) will only take a hyphen until they become familiar. After all, words like wristwatch, flowerpot and weekend all started life in hyphenation land.

Hyphens serve to bring separate words into a single word. If you use 'compound phrases', that is phrases such as day-to-day, up-to-date and in-depth as if they were one word, then hyphenate them, but only if they come before a noun. For example: *The centre's up-to-date records*. But *The centre's records are all up to date*.

> *'The Department is pleased that its co-operation with the voluntary sector has improved over the past year'.*

A hyphen is usually best employed where, as in this example, it separates two of the same letters. Words like *preempt* and *reestablish* look odd without the hyphen. Add one in (*pre-empt, re-establish*) and there's no need to work out what's being said. However, in the above example this may not necessarily be the case for *co-operate*. Modern dictionaries are now comfortable with *cooperate*. It's a tough one to call, but it's your call. However:

> *'Ms McKinney is a co-opted Member of the Social Services Committee'.*

I think this is fine as the alternative *coopted* is unsatisfactory.
The following example gives us three hyphenated words to look at.

> *'Bathrooms and toilets have also been re-furbished and the call-bell system up-dated'.*

There are many examples of people hyphenating words that begin with *re*. Again, your guide must be *will it read okay without the hyphen?* I think *refurbished* can only be read and understood in the way intended, so lose the hyphen. Indeed most *re* words can lose the hyphen just as quickly as a departmental restructure loses jobs. However, where it would result in two *e*'s joining, it's safer to keep the hyphen: *re-elected councillor* rather than *reelected councillor*. Back to the example, call-bell rings a few alarm bells. 'Callbell' is unsatisfactory. 'Call bell' could, unlikely as it may seem, be misinterpreted as a command. 'Call-bell' may be the most appropriate. A hyphen on *updated* is outdated - it's a familiar word now. De-hyphenate. O-kay?

Hyphens are also used to separate statements from the main thread of a sentence. In this way, they are performing the same task as a comma, only more obviously so. The following example is from **Community Care**.

> *'Money - or the lack of it - is the key to problems faced by country folk'.*

Brackets ({[()]})

The posh word for brackets is 'parentheses'. Brackets do the same job as commas and dashes. They can all indicate an aside or some additional or background information. In *The Good English Guide*, Godfrey Howard says that of the three, brackets give you the most separation from the flow of the sentence, commas the least. Thus, the comma could be used for:

> *'The parents believed, it was said, that the pre-school group was much needed'.*

The hyphen could be used for:

> *'The parents believed - with some justifiable conviction - that the pre-school group was much needed'.*

And brackets could be used for:

> *'The parents believed (and nearly 20 turned up to have their say) that the pre-school group was much needed'.*

Dots [...]

The posh word for these dots is ellipsis. This is the use of three dots to signify **and so on** *(Plain English means avoiding long sentences, jargon, big words...)* and indicating that something has been left out from a quote. For example, *The next review will need to look at this issue to see how this has benefited Marcus* could read: *The next review will ... see how this has benefited Marcus.*

The dots can also signify a delay or pause until the next word. But, above all, just remember that like the Musketeers, the Coins in the Fountain, the Amigos, and Days of the Condor, there are but *three* of them...no more, no less.

Speech marks [" ""]

You put speech marks (or inverted commas, quotation marks or quotes) around direct speech. Thus:

> *Noel said 'I want to be able to go on the bus on my own'.*

Also if you are quoting a title:

> *The information booklet on the Nursery contains a statement called 'Our Philosophy'.*

More often in writing for social services it will signify a colloquial phrase. Something like: *'He was obviously 'fed up' and shouted at me again'.* We also use speech marks to highlight buzz words. This fact alone assures their future with us. This means we sit and suffer the following.

- *'These practices have 'impacted' on the dynamics of the home'.*
- *'It's recommended that 'permanency preparation' is implemented'.*
- *'The 'likes' and 'dislikes' of children'.*
- *'It may also be helpful to ask parents 'how' they might like to get involved, you could also explore developing a 'skills' bank'.*

In keeping with the modern trend, all the examples quoted, as is the preferred style of this book, use single speech marks ['...'] rather than double ones ["..."]. Double speech marks are not redundant because the need to use them within single speech marks will save them from the job centre.

> *'Dion enjoys music and reading. He's ordered "Lost in Music" by Giles Smith from his library'.*

One final thing. There are a few schools of thought on where to place the final speech mark: should it be done before or after the full stop, for example? The school this book attends (which some will argue should be named and shamed) is the one that prefers the stop *outside* of the speech marks unless the punctuation is necessarily part of the quote - usually a question or exclamation mark. But for no other reason than I think it looks better. It is a matter of style, after all.

Whichever way you deal from the punctuation pack you should *try* to be consistent but keep a card or two up your sleeve. You should stick with your preferred punctuation style but twist it if you feel it helps your hand. See your speech marks and raise you 20.

Chapter 4

Is it clear?

Is it clear?

'The curtains and blinds are pulled by children.
Staff feel they are old and should be replaced'.

- from an inspection report

Part of the beauty of the English language is its range and flexibility. One word can have several meanings. For example *draw* = draw (a picture), pull, bend, divert, attraction, inhale, extract, extend, move, tie. Also English has a number of words or phrases that basically mean the same thing. For example, cherish, appreciate, value, prize, treasure, think the world of, regard, admire.

You can do so many things with English. You can pun to your art's content. You can play on words without adult supervision. You can beef on about language until the cows come home.

However, this flexibility, dynamism and nuance can also open the language up to confusion and misinterpretation. It's important to make sure that what you write is understood in the way you intended and at the first time of asking.

You need to be aware of troublesome words and clumsy sentence construction that leave your meaning up for grabs. Some words to be wary of include **outstanding** - which is often used to mean *not yet done* but is more often read to mean *brilliant*; **common** - which to some means *shared* or *usual* but to others means a *lack of education or taste*, or *working class* - which doesn't necessarily mean ill-educated; and **presently** - which to some means *in a while* but to others means *now*.

Sometimes the net result is confusion. But amusingly so. I remember seeing a notice outside a hospital saying *'Security dogs operate here'*. Apart from conjuring up in my mind a picture of a Dobermann in mask growling 'Scalpel', it was made all the funnier for being outside a hospital in Barking, Essex. Another canine example is *'Dogs must be carried on the escalator'*. This actually means that you can't go on the escalator unless you are carrying a dog.

Unclear but clearly funny

I've come across several examples of unintentionally funny statements made in social services inspection reports. These have included:

> 'The inspector pointed out a cracked mirror. The manager said he would look into it'.

There's a manager in reflective mood.

> 'None of the residents are capable of managing their own financial affairs. The administrator is to be commended for her efficiency'.

Quite right, too.

> 'The Manager commented that the staff discuss discipline and tactics for dealing with inappropriate behaviour at their staff meetings'.

I'm sure we've all been to staff meetings like that.

> 'Notes are written on each resident at least twice daily'.

Obviously short of paper at this home.

> 'No office as such is available to staff but generous cupboard space is provided, some above child height'.

What more could you seriously ask for?

> '...and also a small resident's kitchen is available next to the main kitchen'.

Undoubtedly equipped with vertically challenged ovens. This is also made even less clear by the misplaced apostrophe on *resident's* when it should be *residents'*.

> 'Recommendation: Arrange for the chiropodist to have sole use of the conservatory when visiting'.

This made me wonder if the home would dig their heels in or keep in step with the recommendation and toe the line which would be some feat.

While I was Head of Inspection at Barking and Dagenham I asked my administrator to keep details of each inspection. This meant recording the date pre-inspection questionnaires were sent out and returned, the number of comments received back from relatives, date of publication of report and so on. This she did efficiently and called the folder *'Breakdown of Inspections'*. To this day, I'm not sure whether she was merely giving the folder its name or making a comment about the effect I had on the service.

Lazy writing

However, not all examples earn a humorous reprieve. Some writing is just lazy or hasn't been that well thought through. This, for example:

> *'It should be ensured that all clients are made aware of their right to complain in writing'.*

Taken at face value this means that clients can't complain verbally but can only do so in writing. This was not the intended meaning. However, a minor change to the word order remedies this.

> *'It should be ensured that all clients are made aware in writing of their right to complain'.*

Another example reads:

> *'There is one lounge area for the use of residents with television and chairs'.*

So if residents don't have a television and some chairs presumably they are barred from using the lounge. Again a simple change in structure makes it clearer.

> *'There is one lounge area with television and chairs for the use of residents'.*

Another example reads:

> *'The proprietors have made their comments and proposals to implement the requirements and recommendations made in the draft report and are reproduced at the end of this report'.*

The proprietors being reproduced at the end of the report? Now that would be worth a look. Change the *'and'* after draft report to *'which'* and confusion is avoided.

'The proprietors have made their comments and proposals
to implement the requirements and recommendations
made in the draft report which are reproduced at the end
of this report'.

A final example reads:

'However, a portable telephone is also available for the
use of both residents and staff'.

The potential confusion here is caused by *both*. This could mean that
the portable phone was only available for two residents (both of them).
The intention was to say it's available for all staff and all residents. However, in this case (and in most others) *both* is unnecessary and should
be avoided.

'However, a portable telephone is also available for the
use of residents and staff'.

Good punctuation

If anything, writing in social services is characterised by over-punctuation
rather than a lack of it. However, there are times when a well-placed
comma comes to the rescue.
For example:

'Whilst accepting that residents should not be prevented
from smoking steps should be taken to prevent the odour
in the building'.

This sentence causes a double take because at first reading it sounds
like residents are *smoking steps* (an under-rated pastime, let me tell you).
A comma placed after *smoking* allows the reader to get to the end of
the sentence without delay. As in:

'Whilst accepting that residents should not be prevented
from smoking, steps should be taken to prevent the odour
in the building'.

And finally...

The last examples in this chapter have a social services connection, and were culled from *Private Eye*. A local South London newspaper printed the headline

> *'Magazine on Tape for Deaf'*.

And finally a public notice:

> *'Poole library will be closed for a week from September 4 to 9 inclusive to make access easier for disabled people'*.

Chapter 5

Away with words

Away with words

'Vigorous writing is concise. A sentence should contain
no unnecessary words, a paragraph no unnecessary sentences,
for the same reason that a drawing should have no unnecessary
lines and a machine no unnecessary parts.
This requires not that the writer make all his sentences short,
or that he avoid the detail and treat his subjects only in outline,
but that every word tell'.

- Professor William Strunk, Jr.

Whatever you write will almost certainly have to compete with other reports or written information. So your reader has to know what it is you're saying and what you want or are offering. In much the same way that the human body is made up of parts that perform some function (except the appendix) so your sentences should only be made up of words that you need. Any extra information should find itself booked into an appendix.

You should omit, leave out and exclude all those unnecessary and needless words and phrases that do not contribute anything to what you have to say and which you don't really need. Or, omit needless words.

The trouble is that we litter pages with words that should never be there and with phrases that have evolved into standard sentence-starters or fillers. We hardly ever question their presence even when they are simply saying the same thing: *first and foremost*, we need to recognise that *each and every* word we use *over and above* those needed should be *null and void*.

It's not always easy sacking words from sentences. The 18th century French poet and critic, Nicolas Boileau, said that of 'every four words I write, I strike out three'. This sounds somewhat obsessional but he was a man on a mission. If you are to edit your own work, the best way is to leave something you have written to one side and come back to it later, re-reading it afresh. If you check something that you've just written the tendency is to gloss over it as you know what's coming. You might also have half a mind on what you are going to write next which is much more exciting than concentrating fully on what you've already written: new pastures always seem to promise more than the old ground.

Hunting out unnecessary words is only the first step towards writing concisely. But it is at times surprising the number of words that can be struck out and still leave the sentence saying the same thing intended by the writer. Therein lies the trick: strike out the words but keep the meaning.

The most common examples in social services writing tend to come from three barely distinguishable groups:

- saying the same thing twice;

- overstating the obvious; and

- saying nothing.

Saying the same thing twice

Strangely, this mistake is made through lazy writing or by trying too hard. Lazy writing means that certain stock phrases get the call-up because the writer is either copying a style of writing that seems acceptable or can't think of anything to say and hopes that something will just come along. Trying too hard means that a writer is wary that certain words might not cover all aspects of what needs to be said. More often than not they're misguided. Here are a few examples with suggested wasted words in bold:

- *'Placement agreements **which** are amended **and modified** on a regular basis'*.

- *'Our complaints procedure has been **revised and** updated'*.

- *'All records were in good order **and well maintained'**.*

- *'Many of the residents' bedrooms have been decorated and furnished to **individual** personal tastes'*.

- *'Until recently, **staffing has been consistent and** there have been few staff changes'*.

Overstating the obvious

This is the 'sky above us' syndrome. Of course it's above us. Obviously. So why say it? It can be amusing to read at times but it can also be irritating. It can also have a detrimental effect on what you are writing as the reader then thinks that what you have to say isn't worth reading. They can belittle your argument or soften the impact of anything critical you may be saying. Here are some examples:

- 'The **text of the** statement highlights choice in a number of areas'.
- 'Activities are planned **in advance** and this is good practice'.

I don't think we normally plan things after they happen, do we? No, that's a Director's job.

- 'It stands in its own grounds and has extensive views of the **local** countryside'.
- 'The playgroup is **situated** in the same building as the **local** primary and nursery school'.
- '**Externally** car parking is provided'.
- 'Is there a **vertical** lift shaft in the home?'
- '...to protect residents, and staff, from **unwanted** intruders'.
- 'Gravy boats were **present** on each table'.

And correct, no doubt.

Saying nothing

This is usually the biggest culprit. All too often we use words that bring nothing to the sentence except increasing the word count. I've listed *below some* examples of the *type of* words to avoid *where possible.*

- 'The living room is **located** on the ground floor'.
- 'The information **contained** in this report'.
- 'It was evident that progress has been made **with regard to** reviewing care plans'.

- *'There are no plans **at present** for staff to attend any courses in the coming year'.*
- *'The alarm is tested **regularly** every three months'.*
- *'Two residents were **in the process of** making preparations to move out'.*
- *'If **in the event that** this is not possible, the manager would be contacted'.*
- *'Staffing remains **completely** unchanged'.*

There are three things you can do to tighten up your writing: edit, edit and edit. You should learn the value of rewriting - although you might feel that time might not permit overindulgence. However, a well written and understood letter or report will save acres of time in the long term.

Invest the time now. The only difficulty with rewriting is the proof reading part. There is a simple truth: when it comes to your own writing, you are the world's worst proof reader. Try to either do it very carefully (avoiding the *I-know-what's-coming skimming technique*) or get somebody else to do it. On second thoughts, *always* get someone else to do it.

It will seem like hard work. But as Dr Samuel Johnson said: *'What is written without effort is in general read without pleasure'*. And you can't fault the boy Johnson.

Padding

Padding

The slight irony of having this, the second of two chapters, to talk about being concise in what you have to say, is not lost on me. It's ignored but not lost. However, I want to emphasise the difference to spotting words that just don't need to be there and spotting wordy phrases, known as *padding*, that may be replaced with shorter alternatives.

I'm sure that padding was invented by those nice people who sell the rest of the world ink and toner. It keeps them in holidays. The more we pad the greater their chance of that nice little retirement bungalow on the Isle of Wight.

Padding is taking the scenic route to making a point, preferring the full guided tour every time. Instead of moving economically straight from A to B, the padder will lose their bearings, go off at a tangent, go around the houses, beat about the bush for a time, and by so doing will bypass the point. Padding is like this paragraph.

In writing for the public you must bear in mind that in the 1990s most people spend their lives in the fast lane. So if you want to avoid people giving your information the hard shoulder treatment, you will have to get in there, make your point and get out.

However, this is easier said than done. We store up and roll out yards of stock phrases that we feel comfortable with. While useful at times they are usually overworked or unnecessary. This is particularly the case for phrases that work as 'sentence starters'. Very rarely can we just sit down and write something straight off the reel. Even short letters require thought and planning. Sometimes we hit that mental wall and simply can't find the word, phrase, rhythm or tone we're looking for. Often the hardest thing to do is to get a sentence going. So we resort to an 'old faithful' in the hope that it will rescue our derailed train of thought.

Social services inspectors can be guilty of this. They often resort to phrases like:

- *'During the inspection...'*
- *'The inspector noted that...'*
- *'On the day of inspection...'*

Indeed, *'During the inspection'* clocked up 16 appearances in one report I read. By the end of the report, I felt that the phrase had worked hard enough to be entitled to a long service award.

- *'During the inspection, the inspector met with four of the residents'.*

Take out the sentence starter (and lose the *'of the'* as well) and you're left with:

- *'The inspector met with four residents'.*

If a report is based on what the inspector saw during an inspection, there is no need to keep reminding people of this fact. Somebody won't read *The inspector met with four residents* and wonder if that happened to be during the inspection or a week later or during a chance meeting at Romford dogs. This type of phrase may serve a purpose but it is so rare it might be easier to find a manager who has said 'Sorry, that was my fault'.

On what basis?

I am convinced that the most overworked phrase in social services today is *on a regular basis*. Staff meetings are never held *regularly*, they are, of course, held *on a regular basis*. It's almost as if it's a legal require-ment to include the phrase at least once in everything ever produced by social services in the western hemisphere. Not to do so is punishable by death or by being sent to work (on a permanent basis, naturally) for a Chief Executive's Department, which is much the same thing really. I'm sorry to shatter your illusions about this but you really don't need to use it. Why use four words when one will do? I understand the treachery of my words. But if you wrap yourself in a black flag, light a candle, and lie down in a darkened room for days on end, you can get through this.

Although *on a regular basis* is the ultimate phrase, its extended family make Ma and Pa Walton seem like a childless couple. It seems we need to put everything onto some sort of basis. This is particularly the case for time, when things can take place on anything from an hourly basis, thorough daily, weekly, fortnightly, monthly and calling at all stops to on an annual basis. Other typical examples are:

- on a flexible basis
- on a part time basis
- on a temporary basis
- on an ongoing basis.

However, some have definitely come from the other side of the fence:

- on a health and safety basis
- on a fostering basis
- on a long term residential care basis
- on an announced and unannounced basis
- on an individual or small group basis.

At least *on a daily basis* is preferable to *on a day to day basis* as that only wastes three words, not five.

Stock phrases

The table below lists some examples of stock phrases that can usually be replaced with single words. In each case you will need to take care with the context of what is being said, the tense and whether it's plural or single.

a considerable number of	*many*
a large amount of	*lots, many*
a minimum of	*at least*
are able to	*can*
are not eligible to	*cannot, can't*

by no means	*not*
considerable amount	*lot, many*
despite the fact that	*although*
expressed the view	*said*
for the duration of	*during, while*
formed the view	*believed, thought, understood*
gained the impression that	*felt, thought*
have been identified as being	*are*
have been made aware	*know, learnt*
in addition to the above	*also*
in advance of	*before*
in relation to	*about*
in the event of	*if*
is detailed with	*has, includes*
is in need of	*needs*
it is often the case	*usually*
of the opinion that	*believes, thinks*
on behalf of	*for*
the majority of	*most*
the provision of	*providing*
was found to have	*had*
were aware	*knew*
were found to consist	*consisted*

Examples

This example is from an assessment.

- *'This may be a way of showing Jo's needs are being met'.*

The *'be a way of'* is redundant. However, by just taking it out we are left with a grammatically incorrect sentence. So we need to change *showing* to *show*. This leaves us with:

- *'This may show Jo's needs are being met'.*

Sometimes we shy away from saying it simply and end up adding deadwood. Take these three similar examples from different reports from different inspection units:

- 'The gardens to the front of the Home are attractive and pleasant'.
- 'There is a landscaped garden at the rear of the building'.
- 'There is a small secluded garden at the rear of the Home'.

We've got gardens to the front of us and gardens to the rear of us. Whatever happened to good old fashioned front gardens and back gardens? Also, each writer has felt obliged to give the reader a reminder that it is the home (or **Home** - inspectors do love a capital letter) that they are talking about. Just in case you hadn't seen the cover or something. So those references can go. This leaves us with:

- 'The front gardens are attractive and pleasant'.
- 'There is a landscaped back garden'.
- 'There is a small secluded back garden'.

Over the three examples we've cut down from 35 words to 20. And as any politician worth their salt will tell you that's a word saving of 43% in real terms.

Sometimes we can overstate the issue as this depressingly unsurprising statement shows.

- 'The staff team are all female with the exception of 1 male who is the Manager'.

We can change *with the exception of* for *except*. As there are only two types of gender at the time of going to press, it isn't necessary to spell this out. The word 'team' is redundant. Also, 'all' could be moved in the sentence to replace the opening 'The'. The alternative reads:

- 'All staff are female except the Manager'.

This has more than halved the number of words used.

Too often we use lazy words and phrases that can be summarily dismissed from the sentence. Take these examples:

- 'The residents are involved in helping to prepare meals'.
- 'There are adequate car parking facilities'.

You rarely need to use phrases like 'are involved in' or words like 'facilities'. Minor changes leaves us with:

- *'The residents help to prepare meals'.*
- *'There is adequate car parking'.*

Active and passive voice

One way to cut padding is to prefer what is called the *active voice* of verbs over the *passive voice*. Like many other grammatical categories, because they are based on Latin or Ancient Greek, *voice* is a curious if not abstract concept to us. However, it's probably one of those things that you do everyday but just didn't know that's what they called it.

It's all a matter of, gulp, how a subject relates to an object in a sentence or clause. It's a question of whether you **do** something (*active*) or have something **done** to you (*passive*). Anyway, enough of this attempt to visually impair you with linguistic wizardry and insight: it's probably best just to show you.

Let's use a simple sentence that we can all relate to:

- *'The dog bit the Director of Social Services'.*

This is in the active voice. The subject of a sentence is the person or thing (in this case, the dog) that is doing the action (biting) to the object of the sentence (your beloved leader).

But:

- *'The Director of Social Services was bitten by the dog'.*

This is in the passive voice. The doer of the action (the dog) has become the object of the sentence. In simple terms, it seems to me that if the person or thing doing the action is at the start of the sentence or clause, it's active. If the person or thing doing the action comes at the end of the sentence or clause, it's passive.

The positive by-products of preferring the active voice (or active verbs) to the passive (or passive verbs) are that it usually means you get to use fewer words (two words in the above example) and it helps liven up your writing. Sadly, wishful thinking was behind the above example, so here are some real examples.

Active voice: example 1

- *'The complaint was made on his behalf by his carer'.* (Passive - 10 words)

This just needs turning around.

- *'His carer made the complaint on his behalf'.* (Active - 8 words)

Active voice: example 2

- *'The overall impression gained by the Inspector was... '* (Passive - 8 words)

In this example, our gain is that we can lose 'gained' as well.

- *'The inspector's overall impression was...'* (Active - 5 words)

Active voice: example 3

- *'The thrust of the approach to health care at this home is the preventative approach'.* (Passive - 15 words)

Here we can see that the use of 'thrust' is not only a bit pompous but unnecessary as well. Also, prefer *preventive* to *preventative* as it's the easier to say of these two interchangeable words.

- *'The home takes a preventive approach to health care'.* (Active - 9 words)

Active voice: example 4

- *'The opportunity to speak to several residents was taken during the inspection'.* (Passive - 12 words)

In this instance by bringing in the person (the inspector) rather than the process (inspection), we can comfortably delete 'the opportunity ...was taken'. This means we halve our word count again.

- *'The inspector spoke to several residents'.* (Active - 6 words)

When to use passive verbs

However, there is a role for passive verbs. This book, for example, because of its discursive style makes quite a use of passive verbs. Indeed, my grammar checker tells me that 15% of my sentences are passive. But this suits the aim of the book to be informally persuasive. So that's all right then.

You should prefer the passive if you feel the active verb is *too hostile* or if you want to *spread responsibility*.

Too hostile

Sending out a letter that says:

> *'We will cancel your registration unless you pay the inspection fee'*

is confrontational. It might be better and less threatening to prefer the passive:

> *'Your registration fee may be cancelled if you do not pay your inspection fee.'*

Spread responsibility

Sometimes (most times? all the time?) we don't too much like putting our hands up and saying 'yeah, it was me, I got it wrong, sorry, it's a fair cop, guv,' and so on. So we prune the active, plant the passive and allow ourselves to come up smelling of roses. For example:

> *'I made a mistake with the date of your assessment'*

is far too honest for some. Blame is shifted with the more passive:

> *'A mistake was made with the date of your assessment'.*

In the Irangate trial, Colonel Oliver North spoke almost exclusively in passive terms - never personally admitting anything - making full use of phrases like *it was clearly indicated* and *it was already known*. So, if someone tries to accuse you of gun-running for your department, you can't say you weren't ever told how to field those tricky questions.

Putting it all together

In the final four examples we will look to use the guidance given in this and the last chapter. In each case the task is to reduce the word count without losing the intended meaning.

Putting it all together: example 1

- *Attention has been given to the promotion of homely surroundings through the use of appropriate decor and furnishings.* (18 words)

What's being said? The home is homely. It has homely decor and furnishings. Homely atmosphere.

- *The decor and furnishings promote a homely atmosphere.* (8 words)

Putting it all together: example 2

- *Although the outward appearance of the Home is somewhat different to others in the road, it still retains ordinary and domestic characteristics.* (22 words).

What's being said? The home *is* different from the outside to others in street. But is still like a normal house.

- *From outside the home looks different to others, but it still looks like an ordinary house.* (16 words)

Putting it all together: example 3

- *Each resident is allocated a key to the front door for their personal use.* (14 words).

What's being said? Each resident has their own front door key. Er, that's it.

- *Each resident has their own front door key.* (8 words)

Putting it all together: example 4

- *Inspectors were informed that a separate handbook intended for parents was in the final stages of preparation. (17 words).*

What's being said? A handbook for parents is being done. It will be finished soon. 'Finished' can sound negative. Also, why say 'Inspectors were informed that...'? If they weren't informed how else would they know?

- *A separate handbook for parents will be ready soon. (9 words)*

And finally...

However, it's only fair to say that padding can have a positive use. Indeed, a social work student pointed out this fact to me during a lecture. Twelve words **are** preferable to three when you're struggling to reach the required 4,000 words in an assignment. I acknowledge your feelings.

Chapter 7

Everyday words

Everyday words

'We should constantly use the most common, little, easy words (so they are pure and proper) which our language affords'.

- John Wesley (from 'Of preaching to plain people')

This sounds daft but it's true: it's hard to write simple English. It seems that once we start to write, words that we rarely speak suddenly start appearing before us. And, distressingly, people seem to think that's how it *should* be done.

There seems to be something evil at work here. In our minds we are terrorised by the need to use big (or impressive, or posh) words. It's as if we need to make full use of a wide vocabulary so that other, lesser beings than ourselves cannot fail to see just how clever we are. It's almost as if we think that the perceived 'quality' (big words and the like) of a document somehow reflects the importance of the subject and the standing of the writer. It seems that the more complicated and convoluted, the better.

So, we write things we'd never say. Take *ascertain*. Actually, don't just take it - take it outside and thrash it to within an inch of its life. We would never say 'Can I look at your paper to ascertain what's on television?' We would always look to *find out* what was on. So, why write it?

I remember reading a report by an environmental health officer that talked about *the first floor sanitary accommodation*. Whatever happened to the good old *upstairs toilet* (or *lavatory* if you must)? In terms of plain English we need to blow the trumpet for the simple and the everyday. This chapter is a fanfare for the commonplace.

So give the cold shoulder to *refrigerator* and chill out with *fridge*; give lip service to *conversing* and chat up *talking*; run a million miles from *adjacent* but snuggle up to *next to*; return *despatched* to sender and deliver *sent out*; disconnect the *water outlets* and turn on the *taps*.

Inspectorspeak

Social services inspectors have their own curious way of saying things. Issues are always *addressed* and never *tackled*. Recommendations are always *implemented* and never *carried out*. Staff and residents always *state* things, and never *say* anything. Records are always *maintained* and never *kept*. Medication is always *administered*, never *given out*. Redecoration takes place throughout *the interior and exterior* of homes, never *inside and out*. And finally, nothing ever happens *before* an inspection but always *prior to* one. For those of you (and you are many) who use *'prior to'* instead of *'before'*, I'm drawn to the comment made by Theodore Bernstein. He said that if you would say *'posterior to'* for *'after'*, then please continue to say *'prior to'* for *'before'*.

We're buzzing

Social work has convinced itself it's a profession. It's important, you see. And in keeping with most professions, social services have a seemingly obsessive need to create and overuse buzz words. We use these words - like *provision, facility* and *resource* - even when (specially when?) the words add nothing to the sentence. They should be left out or replaced with something more specific. Another tendency is to use a word like *incorporated* (*'the client's unmet needs are incorporated into their file'*) when what is really meant is *included*. Or to say *developed* (*'a complaints procedure should be developed'*) when what is really meant is *written*.

An inspector reported on a visit to a nursery:

> *'The building was commissioned four years ago'*.

It seems a fairly straightforward, harmless little sentence. Unfortunately, the inspector incorrectly chose 'commissioned' to mean *opened*. By looking for a bigger, more impressive word the inspector changed the meaning. You should try to keep it simple. Also, it's a report on a nursery so why avoid the specific for the general? If the nursery was only part of the building (a family centre, say) then the use of 'building' would be justifiable. However, it was a purpose built nursery. If it's a nursery, call it a nursery and throw *building, facility, resource, centre, daycare provision* and other assorted titles out of your pram.

Also, the phrase 'four years ago' is relative and could easily mislead. Inspection reports may be available to the public over many years. So what *was* four years ago at the time of writing, simply isn't now. It's better to put the specific date (in this case 1990). So the plainer version would read:

> *'The nursery opened in 1990'.*

It's shorter, easier to understand, more specific and it's now accurate.

Keep with the familiar

I believe we should write more like we talk. This is not to say that we should come over all colloquial but we should look to communicate with people with words that they are familiar with.

My *Shorter Oxford English Dictionary* tells me that the English word for having a style characterised by the use of long words is *sesquipedalianism*. I think that's great. Let's use a great big eight syllable word to describe the practice of overusing great big words. I'll subscribe (with my own money) to that. I'm not sure what the plain alternative to *sesquipedalianism* could be but I reckon 'Have you swallowed a dictionary or what?' might not be too far off beam.

Examples

This first example is taken from a social services department's application form.

- *'References are always sought prior to commencing employment'.*

By using more everyday words, it could have read:

- *'References are always taken up before you start working for us'.*

You might think that this appears to occur frequently. You would be right. But it seems to happen a lot, as well. Here's some proof.

- *'Locks have been fitted for the residents who have requested this facility'.*

In everyday words:

- *'Locks have been fitted for the residents who have asked for them'.*

- *'...as well as their role in maintaining accurate, pertinent and current records appertaining to the well being of the service user'.*

In everyday words:

- *'...as well as their role to keep accurate, relevant and up-to-date records on the well being of the service user'.*

- *'Can admission to the nursery be effected without ringing the bell?'*

In everyday words:

- *'Can people get into the nursery without ringing the bell?'*

- *'Clients have appropriate access to documentation maintained about them'.*

In everyday words:

- *'Clients can see their own files'.*

Formal words and their everyday alternatives

Listed below are words and phrases taken from written English produced by social services departments. In some cases the suitability of the alternative depends on the context.

Formal words	Everyday words
a maximum of	*up to*
a viable option	*possible*
accessible to children	*within the reach of children*
accommodated	*living, lived*
according to our records	*our records show*
ad hoc	*now and then, as and when*
adhered to	*kept to*
amongst	*among, within*
appended to the report	*at the back of the report*
approximately	*about*
are commensurate with	*reflect, equal*
assist	*help*
attempt	*try*
bi-annual	*twice a year*
bi-ennial	*every two years*
close proximity	*nearby, close to*
commence	*start, begin*
complete	*finish, fill in*
comply with	*keep to, meet*
concurred	*agreed*
contained	*had*
contained within	*in*
demonstrate	*show*
denotes	*is*
designated	*named, appointed*
despatched	*sent out*
determine	*find out*
discrete	*separate*
discuss	*talk about*
documentation	*paperwork, papers, documents*
eg, exempli gratia	*for example, for instance*
endeavour	*try*
endorse	*agree with, support*
enhance	*improve*

erected	*put up*
established in 1989	*set up in 1989*
etc (*et cetera*)	*and so on*
exhibit	*have, show*
expenditure	*spending*
express their view	*have their say*
facilitate	*make possible, help*
factor	*reason*
factually correct	*true*
forename	*first name*
forthwith	*from now on*
General Practitioner	*GP, doctor*
henceforth	*from now on*
ie, (*id est*)	*that is (to say)*
impacted	*affected*
inspect	*look at*
installed	*fitted*
is operated by	*is run by*
location of establishment	*address*
London Fire and Civil Defence Association (or LFCDA)	*fire brigade*
maintained	*kept*
modify	*change*
more audible	*louder*
NB, nb (*nota bene*)	*please note*
nearing completion	*nearly finished*
numerous	*many*
objective	*aim, goal*
obtained	*got*
out of commission	*out of order*
participate	*take part*
per annum	*each year, every year, yearly*
persons	*people*
preceding twelve months	*(during the) last year*
predominantly	*mainly, largely*
prescribed	*set, fixed*

previous	*last*
principal	*main*
prior to	*before*
pro-forma	*form*
proprietor	*owner*
purchased	*bought*
reciprocated	*shown in return*
rectified	*put right*
regarding	*about*
reimbursed	*paid, refunded*
relocating	*moving*
requested	*asked*
reside	*live*
residential accommodation	*home*
residing	*living*
respite care residents	*short stay residents*
retail outlets	*shops*
seat restraints	*seat belts*
self administer	*take their own*
statutory	*legal*
subsequent	*next*
subsequently	*later*
to become accustomed to	*to get used to*
twelve month period	*year*
undertaken	*carried out*
utilise	*use*
via	*by*
water outlets	*taps*
whereas	*but*
whilst	*while*
with respect to	*about*

The next time you write something, look at it carefully. Be honest with yourself and pick out each time you use official or pompous words instead of their everyday alternatives. Change them. Then read it again and see how many you missed first time around.

And remember, if at first you don't succeed, endeavour, endeavour again.

Chapter 8

Shortening sentences

Shortening sentences

Size is important.

What is a sentence?

A sentence has been described in the following ways:

- a set of words expressing a complete thought
- a sentence has a 'subject' (= the topic) and a 'predicate' (= what is being said about the topic)
- a sentence is a group of words that must normally include a finite verb and must normally form a complete unit communication
- sentences are units made up of one or more clauses.

The 'set of words expressing a complete thought' is perhaps the most quoted definition. However, it is ultimately unsatisfactory as it leads to problems in defining what a *thought* is. These days linguists shy away from defining a sentence. An entry in *The Oxford Companion to the English Language* takes about a thousand words to admit that 'the sentence is notoriously difficult to define'.

As far as this book is concerned, we're going to bed with a sentence being the stuff between full stops. That's full stops as in full stops, exclamation marks and question marks. I realise this definition is flawed, particularly for some Asian languages that don't make use of full stops. But as this book is specifically about plain English and not plain language it suits my purpose. So, this is a sentence. So's this. And this.

Why should we keep sentences short?

Without wishing to put too fine a technical point on it, I believe short sentences are good and long sentences are bad. Unlike the Tory line - or New Labour's come to that - on penal reform, this book suggests the shortening of sentences. How often have you read something only to realise that you haven't taken in what's being said and had to go back to the start of a sentence or paragraph? It's more than likely that the sentence you were reading was complex or convoluted and you simply lost the thread. In short, it was too long.

When reading, people store information in their brain. Once the information is complete it is deposited safely in the memory bank. If a sentence carries a number of pieces of information, we can't box them away until the sentence is completed. However, sometimes with long sentences our concentration becomes focused on simply getting to the end of a sentence that we don't pay full attention to what is being said.

This is not to suggest that every sentence should be short in a *Janet and John* or *Rosie and Jim* type of way. For example:

- *The home is small. It is in the community. It is called Telfer House. It has five residents. They all have learning disabilities. They are all men.*

This is very easy to understand. But it's also very dull to read. This rat-a-tat approach should be avoided. Each sentence has one piece of information. However, this type of information is manageable in larger portions. The above example could read:

- *Telfer House is a small community home for people with learning disabilities. The home's five residents are all men.*

This reads better and is still easy to understand.

Newspapers and sentence length

Newspapers provide good examples in contrasting styles. Broadsheets like *The Independent* or *The Guardian* will not think twice about printing 30 plus word sentences. Their target audience is largely an educated one, so this presents no problems. Tabloids like *The Sun* and *Daily Star* would not think once about printing such long sentences. Their target audience prefers things put in an easy-to-read way. Here's how two papers reported incidents during the Iraq crisis on 6 February 1998.

- *'If Iraq is bombed again, they argue, it will strengthen President Saddam. The Secretary-General of the French foreign ministry, Betrand Dufourcq, was in Baghdad*

> *yesterday trying to find a diplomatic settlement acceptable to both Baghdad and the US. French officials say they believe that Iraq is shifting its ground, but they accept that President Saddam must acknowledge the fundamental principle of free access to all possible arms sites for inspectors of the UN's choice'.* **The Independent.**

- *'Defence chiefs plan to drop a circle of bombs around Baghdad in a bid to topple Saddam. Military leaders in Britain and America want to isolate him by cutting links to the capital. They hope that will let opposition groups in Iraq launch a revolt. And rebels would be given Allied backing to ensure Saddam is finally ousted. The plan emerged as Foreign Secretary Robin Cook arrived in the Gulf to rally support for air strikes'.* **The Sun.**

The Independent's piece used 74 words with its three sentences running to 12, 26 and 36 words. This gave an average sentence length of 24.7 words. The Sun's piece used 76 words with its five sentences running to 17, 16, 12, 13, and 18 words. But each sentence averaged 15.2 words.

As a guide, I would suggest that you look to average between 15 and 20 words per sentence. The important word here is *average*. I'm not suggesting that you shouldn't write 30 word sentences if they're essential, easy to follow and make sense. Writing is more effective if sentence length is varied. It's more lively and is more likely to keep the reader's attention.

If information is delivered in snatches it is easier to take in and understand. This will sometimes mean a sentence will only have one piece of information. Sometimes there might be more but this should always be manageable amounts of information. If people struggle to understand what you've written first time then that might just be your fault not theirs.

How to shorten your sentences

On reading back something you've written you notice a long and winding sentence that you can't read in one breath (a sound scientific test).

It obviously needs to be cut up but what do you do? First, you could look at your punctuation. This will usually mean commas, less so colons and semi-colons. Second, you could also look out for words like *and, but, however,* and *although.* Words like these and your punctuation may give you opportunities to cut your sentence down to size.

Replacing commas with full stops

Where you see a comma, there's a good chance that you can use a full stop. As in the following examples.

- 'A staff training booklet is available but is rarely used, the format in this booklet needs to be revised to include induction of new staff'.

- 'Some residents say they enjoy village life, they are well known and a few have struck up individual friendships with neighbours, others feel they are open to public scrutiny and find this intrusive'.

Simply change the commas in both examples to full stops.

- 'A staff training booklet is available but is rarely used. The format in this booklet needs to be revised to include induction of new staff'.

- 'Some residents say they enjoy village life. They are well known and a few have struck up individual friendships with neighbours. Others feel they are open to public scrutiny and find this intrusive'.

In the first example a 25 word sentence becomes two sentences of 10 and 15 words with an average length of 12.5 words. In the second example a 33 word sentence becomes three sentences of 7, 14 and 12 words with an average length of 11 words.

Sometimes if you change a comma to a full stop you will need to change or add in words to help the new sentence make sense. As in the following example.

- 'All review participants were concerned that Family Placements chose not to send a representative to the

> *Review, given the agreement by Panel that he should be found a permanent placement, and that the Review recommendation which had been supported by Family Placements at the last Review, indicated that he needed an urgent family placement'.*

This 54 word monster certainly needs slaying. However, as you can see in this case we can't simply replace commas for full stops. We can put full stops in for the first two commas as these pauses bring us to a natural close. But we need to rework the start of the new sentences. We can't put a full stop in for the last comma as it would stop the thread of the sentence. Indeed we need to **add in** a comma before *which* as '*which had been supported by Family Placements at the last Review*' is an aside to the main information in the sentence. We need to recognise this with punctuation.

With the first comma now a full stop we need to restart the sentence. We could add in '*This is specially so*' or '*Particularly so*'. With the second comma also now a full stop we should perhaps prefer '*Also*' to '*And*'. This leaves us with:

- *'All review participants were concerned that Family Placements chose not to send a representative to the Review. Particularly so given the agreement by Panel that he should be found a permanent placement. Also that the Review recommendation, which had been supported by Family Placements at the last Review, indicated that he needed an urgent family placement'.*

The 54 word dog has now been broken up into 17, 15 and 24 word puppies. The average length is now 18 words.

Picking out conjunctions

This next example shows how we can shorten sentences by picking out conjunctions - words that link other words or other groups of words together.

- *'Some opportunities were available for residents to pursue leisure activities both in the home and in the local community but some residents and/or their relatives commented that there could be more stimulation and activity in the home'.*

This sentence runs to 37 words and is only giving us two pieces of information. The only natural break is provided by *but* - which joins the two pieces of information together. There's a widespread belief that you can't start sentences with words like *but*. But you can. And *The Oxford English Dictionary* has no problems doing it, so why should we? Provided your sentence reads well and makes sense, you can start it with any word you like.

I have just argued that using *but* at the start of a sentence is fine. But in the above example I think it would be better replaced with *However*, which is probably a 'warmer' word. I like to use *However* as it provides an excellent lead-in to a sentence or paragraph. So by changing just one word of the writer's original we should be able to improve the readability of the piece.

- *'Some opportunities were available for residents to pursue leisure activities both in the home and in the local community. However, some residents and/or their relatives commented that there could be more stimulation and activity in the home'.*

Even though it's more readable, there are a few things I would also change in the example. The word *'both'* used in the sense here is redundant - take it out and you lose nothing from the sentence. Similarly, we could lose *'local'* as the meaning is implicit in the sentence. The use of *'and/or'* is lazy, clumsy and ugly (not necessarily in that order). In the sense meant here, *'and'* would adequately replace *'and/or their'*. I would also prefer *'said'* to *'commented'* and replace *'more stimulation and activity'* with a simpler *'more things to do'*. This leaves us with:

- *'Some opportunities were available for residents to pursue leisure activities in the home and in the local community. However, some residents and relatives said that there could be more things to do in the home'.*

According to the Flesch formula, this third version is nearly three times more readable than the original.

Minor rewriting

Sometimes a simple substitution of words is not enough and some minor rewriting helps. Take this example.

- *'The home uses few household remedies eg paracetamol, hot lemon, and honey, and it was stated if residents refuse medication other forms would be used eg liquids, and the General Practitioner would be informed if the situation continued'.*

First of all, it's better to avoid using Latin words and their abbreviations (most commonly *etc*, *ie* and *eg*). They are not as well understood as thought by some people. Even people who use them often get *ie* and *eg* confused. So avoid all potential confusion and write them out in full. But in English not Latin.

You may well find that *'for example'* is a useful phrase to start a sentence with. In the example above we can do this for the first *'eg'* used. The second is a bit clumsy and could help the general flow of the text if it was moved in the sentence and replaced with *'such as'*.

Again we can bring sentences to an end where we find commas and words like *'and'*. In this case they can just be deleted. Also, *'General Practitioner'* can be struck off in favour of *'GP'* or *'doctor'*. The phrase 'household remedies' (and even the more usual 'homely remedies') might cause people outside of social and health care a dry, tickly confusion. It might be better to soothe their worries with 'non-prescription medicines'. Some other phrases have also been replaced with more everyday ones. A rewrite could give us:

- *'The home uses some non-prescription medicines. For example, paracetamol, hot lemon, and honey. It was said that if residents refuse their medication, other forms - such as liquids - would be used. The doctor would be informed if the situation continued'.*

Again, according to the Flesch formula, this is three times more readable.

Using lists

Occasionally you may find that even after shortening your sentences the information you are trying to put across could still seem unclear or difficult for your reader. Sometimes a list might be your answer. This 68 word sentence that would clearly benefit from being put into a list.

- *This is considered to be an "invasion of the body" technique and may only be carried out by Home staff if the resident's doctor has given clear instructions, the staff member is appropriately trained, and prepared to carry out the procedure, the resident or advocate gives their consent and all such training instruction and permissions are clearly recorded on each resident's care plan and every administration is recorded'.*

Given the nature of this 'instruction' it would be difficult to get the whole picture and such a lot of information needs to be presented in a clearer way, which has little to do with the words used, but rather how it is presented. A list would turn this into:

This is considered to be an "invasion of the body" technique. It may only be carried out by Home staff if:

- *the resident's doctor has given clear instructions*
- *the staff member is appropriately trained and prepared to carry out the procedure*
- *the resident or advocate gives their consent*
- *all such training instruction and permissions are clearly recorded on each resident's care plan*
- *every administration is recorded.*

This makes the information much easier to understand.

Oh and just in case you were wondering, even with the long winded examples in this chapter I still averaged 14.9 words a sentence. And the whole book averaged 14.5 words a sentence. So there.

Chapter 9

Jargon and social services speak

DIRECTORATE OF INCOMPREHENSI-
BILIZATION AND INTER-RELATED
NON-ELUCIDATORY OBFUSCANTILIZATION

Jargon and
social services speak

> 'Even between experts, jargon is used to cover up half-baked thoughts
> or to make the commonplace sound important and significant'.

> - Godfrey Howard

Jargon is the curse of the modern age. However, it is not a modern phenomenon. Its exact origin is unknown but the word jargon was used in the 14th century. It meant the meaningless chattering and twittering of birds. Although jargon does have a legitimate role to play, it is best known today for its abuse rather than its use.

A useful shorthand

At best, jargon is a useful shorthand that enables prompt, clear and concise communication between those who understand it. Social workers and residential care workers talking or writing to each other are presumably on safe ground with phrases like *dependency levels, challenging behaviour* and *keyworker systems*. As are nursery workers who might talk about the *developmental stages* of children, *gross* and *fine motor skills*, or the advantages of *age-related base groups*.

Even a 1998 Dartington social research unit brochure for a seminar on 'Post Children Act research' might mean something to the strategic planners and senior managers, whose departmental training budgets Dartington clearly wants to access. The brochure claimed in all its academic glory that '*new Children's Services Plans are being fashioned, with an emphasis on needs-led services, evidence based practice and multi-agency approaches*'. If they put it more simply, quite simply their target audience might not think it much cop.

For jargon to be successful it needs all people to be in on the act. This legitimate use of jargon is a sad and distant second to its abuse.

The abuse of jargon

It is when people feel crowded out by the in-crowd that jargon stops being a shorthand and becomes confusing and frustrating. If someone makes an enquiry to social services should it necessarily follow that they will have an automatic handle on *care management and assessment procedures, user empowerment* or *multi-disciplinary and multi-agency approaches?* Of course not.

When jargon is used to impress, exclude or is just used unthinkingly, it is inconsiderate communication. Jargon is all too often used to make simple, everyday ideas sound more impressive by pumping them up with the air of authority. So rather than talk about pubs, libraries and sports centres we talk about *community facilities.* And a simple idea like *working together with others* is hijacked and forced to land in the weasel-words world of managementspeak. So we get: '*It should be recognised that accessing partnerships would provide a useful and timely opportunity to map out and strengthen outcome-driven joint visions*'.

At the moment it seems social services departments are flooded with macho-drenched business-speak. And sadly rather than washing their hands of it, managers are taking to the waters.

A kick in the teeth

While jargon earns a crust from social services, it manages to rear its ugly head almost everywhere. For example, I've yet to be convinced by the pseudo-scientific approach to toothpaste adverts on television. I'll carry on using the brand I've always used whether or not it promises 'ultra cavity protection'. And I'll brush each day oblivious to the fact that its unique calcium and fluoride formula is fighting the plaque acids that cause cavities. However, on inspection of the tube I am concerned that it contains only two types of ingredient: *'active and other'* (presumably inactive?). However, this is quickly outweighed by the knowledge that it also contains dicalcium phosphate dihydrate. Well, that's all right then.

Advertising has hit a rich vein of jargon. We can all make it through each day in the knowledge that beauty creams, on the face of it, will make full use of anti-occidents to neutralise free radicals. I don't know about you, but I used to wake up with cold sweats in the middle of the night, anxious that my free radicals might not yet be fully neutralised.

Any sport in a storm

All things have their own language - some more accessible than others. For some football has become the it-sport of the nineties. Inevitably it has its own vocabulary: that which is fairly common (*offside, hat trick, own goal, sick as a parrot*) and that which is more specific (*early doors, back door, route one, down the channels, flat back four*).

Indeed social services in what seems to resemble a last throw of the dice attempt to justify its existence in the mean, streamlined, flatter, fitter business-oriented world has adopted some hip (that is, American) sports imagery. We now *touch base, quote ballpark figures, move goalposts* on increasingly *uneven playing fields*, and *pick things up while running behind others*. We can also *bat for the team, kick for goal,* and still be home in time for tea.

Does not compute

But perhaps the most notorious jargon at the time of writing is that related to information technology or IT. Or *computers* to you and me. Okay, IT is more than just computers (faxes, tv's and so on are grouped under it) but when people talk about IT the listeners generally understand it to mean computers. Anybody born before 1980 is at an immediate disadvantage (or ID).

The council I used to work for changed the name of its *Computer Section* to the more grand *Information and Systems Technology Division*. It somehow feels more appropriate. The thing with computer jargon is not just its existence but the sheer size and power of it. You've got applications, boilerplates, RAM, megabytes, navigating on-line with jumps (which admittedly sounds worth exploring), mouse pointers, and dragging and dropping. You can activate, create and modify. You can set fields, wrap text, load add-ins, mail merge, filter records, customise toolbars, shrink to fit, run macros and link data.

The newness of computers means a whole new language stalking the planet. It may be unfair to label all the above examples as jargon, as a boilerplate might well be dead common in a few years' time. But I reckon the language is still a mystery to most.

When I was planning to buy my first computer in 1996, I took care to read up on the subject first. I figured if I was to part with the best part of £2,000 (or *2K* as we say) then I wanted to have a choice that was, in part at least, informed. I chose to read the magazines claiming to talk the layperson's talk. Even so, I still felt they were taking it as read that the reader would have some knowledge of the subject.

Trips to computer stores very quickly declined to zero. Spotty youths (who had obviously lied about their age and were clearly playing truant) masqueraded as shop assistants and spoke a language that I was simply ill-equipped to be part of in any way, shape or form. The language seemed specification-oriented. I don't need to know how a tv works before I buy one but I do need to know what it can do and how. The same with computers. I bought my computer mail order in the end. And guessed the specification.

It was a frustrating experience that disincluded me, made me feel inadequate and confused. Those who know me may say that's not too difficult to achieve, but I think you know what I mean.

Off the shelf

However, it seems a conspiracy (albeit a welcome one) is afoot to out-date this book even before it goes to press. Computer magazines - given such a hard time above - have gone plain English crazy. It seems they are out to take mega-bites out of my arguments and ram them down my enhanced parallel port.

In March 1998, at least three magazines appeared on the geek shelves at all good newsagents: *Windows Made Easy* ('All you need to know about Windows explained in English' - which is probably a treat a long time in coming for all glaziers); *P C Basics* ('Written for beginners. By experts. In plain English.' No doubt a positive boon to all beat bobbies); and *Computer Active* ('New! 99p Only' - well, it didn't advertise its plain English credentials on the cover of the issue I bought, although its radio advertising campaign centred on them).

The first two named seemed to me have a peculiar notion as to the stuff of plain English. One of them explained helpfully that I could play games on the internet thanks to 'Internet Explorer 4's extensive support of key internet standards such as Dynamic HTML, Java, and the Channel Definition Format'. The other tells me how 'information transferral rates are measured' and that the 'term "PC" is also commonly used to describe an "IBM compatible" personal computer in contra-distinction to an Apple Macintosh computer'.

The third magazine, *Computer Active*, is very good. Each article has its own 'jargonbuster' box. It also makes great use of words like *we've, our, your*, and contractions like *can't, won't* and so on which help readability. It also has the distinction (notably without the *contra*) of being awarded a crystal mark by Plain English Campaign. *Computer Active* is probably as good as this type of magazine can get for making the world of computers orbit somewhere close to planet Earth.

The Hafli experience

A more relevant experience happened to me in 1991. I had recently been appointed Head of Inspection at Barking and Dagenham and was attending a meeting of heads of units from other London boroughs. They kept referring to something called *'Hafli'*. Everyone would nod in agreement at its very mention. I had no idea what hafli was, is, or aspired to. So, I did exactly what any reasonable, self-respecting person in my position would do - I pretended I knew what it was. I nodded away with the best of them, in agreement that hafli was without doubt the best thing since ciabatta with sundried tomatoes. Well, they were a deeply middle class bunch.

As the meeting wore on, I was gradually worn down. Taking the risk of seeming ignorant, not very good at my job, plain stupid or all six, I piped up: 'Excuse me, I know this might sound stupid, but what's hafli?' Thankfully I was spared the feared finger-pointing ridicule and was matter-of-factly informed that it was the Department of Health's publication 'Homes Are For Living In'. Indeed it was a document I knew, and in fact had in front of me at the meeting. I just did not know it by its acronym. Jargon has that effect on you - it can belittle you, make you feel inadequate and cut you off. A lesson was learnt. And a salutary one at that.

Where legals dare

The language of law (legalese) is another area that is over-complicated by jargon. Legalese is characterised by complex and wordy structures causing it to be pompous and dull. Until the 14th century all laws were written in Latin or French. Both these influences distressingly live on today.

Defenders of legalese (although, of course, they would never call it that) argue that legal documents must be written to ensure clarity and leave no room for ambiguity. Witness the following: 'The truth, the whole truth and nothing but the truth'. Someone swearing just to tell 'the truth' leaves room to wriggle, obviously. Defenders will also bang on about the need for confidence in the system and that these legal formulations have been tried and tested without let or hindrance, as it were, over centuries. However, there may be hope. *Clarity* is an organisation set up by British lawyers to campaign for plainer legal English. The Treasury has also recruited tax lawyers to help rewrite Britain's tax laws in plain English. Let's hope this is but the start.

I fail to see how junking phrases like *inter alia, null and void* and *without prejudice* will bring down the legal system as we know it. It might help make things like contracts easier for people to understand and reduce the causes of unnecessary anxiety and confusion.

The mischievous or cynical (or anyone else come to that) might find the argument that the over-complication of language is essential to make it crystal clear is somewhat hard to wash. They might think that the real reason legal documents are so baffling is that it means that we have to retain lawyers to explain it all to us. This means that lawyers remain indispensable, their profession is protected and, of course, the cheques keep rolling in. What do you call a lawyer at the bottom of the ocean? A start.

In sickness and in health

I think that recently, the health service has become a worse offender than social services. I remember the days of GPs, doctors and health visitors. Now we have *primary health care services*. There appears to be a direct link between the increase in the use of health-related jargon and the increase in health service managers coupled with the decrease in front line resources. All they are doing is putting up the protective 'we know best' shutters.

However, not all health jargon is designed to show off the importance of the health service or to save jobs. Some of it is just plain daft. For example, there's the celebrated NHS circular which defined a bed as: '*a device or arrangement that may be used to permit a patient to lie down when the need to do so is a consequence of the patient's condition rather than a need for active intervention such as examination, diagnostic intervention, manipulative treatment, obstetric delivery or transport*'. Annual awards are held by Plain English Campaign for the best and worst examples of public information. The booby prize is called a Golden Bull award. You won't be shocked to learn that the NHS's definition of a bed won a Golden Bull.

Examples of jargon commonly used by social services departments

- *accessibility*
- *admission criteria*
- *age related base groups*
- *age-appropriate*
- *care management*
- *care packages*
- *care planning*
- *care provision*
- *challenging behaviour*
- *child-centred*
- *community facilities*
- *community health practitioner*
- *complex needs assessment*
- *continuity of care*
- *core criteria*
- *delivery of care*
- *dependency levels*
- *developmental stages*
- *domiciliary care agencies*
- *ethos*
- *gender related issues*
- *induction programmes*
- *interaction*
- *keyworker system*
- *management infrastructure*
- *open reporting*
- *positive holistic approach*
- *primary health care*
- *principles of care*
- *regulatory framework*
- *regulatory requirements*
- *resettlement*
- *resourcing*
- *respite care*
- *social role valorisation*
- *staff supervision*
- *strategic planning*
- *supernumerary*
- *supportive network*
- *value base*

Taking care over jargon

I have said that jargon does have a legitimate use. But sometimes even that is questionable. Just because someone works within the care industry it does not always mean that they understand all the jargon. The word *supervision* means quite different things to different people. In social services departments it is usually well understood to mean 'professional supervision' - where a worker meets in private with a senior worker to check on progress, talk about their work, ideas, training needs, challenges and so on. However, outside of a social services department it rarely means the same thing. I recall a manager of a private care home who when asked 'Do you supervise your staff?' replied 'Well I do pop out and keep an eye on them from time to time'.

We also at times start thinking certain words or phrases are common currency because we have used them in our everyday work for a long time. In 1996 some London boroughs started working together to produce, as they called it, 'a framework for the voluntary accreditation of domiciliary care agencies'. Actually they had the title in capital letters and in bold type, but I didn't want to scare you any more than necessary. While I agreed with the principles, I had a problem with the title. I announced to my borough's Advisory Group that we would be calling our scheme a decidedly lower case 'registration of home care services'.

'I refuse to have anything to do with the phrase *domiciliary care*,' I said, chest expanding with the virtue of plain English. 'In this borough people know it as home care, and that's what we're going to call it'. One of our members of the public on the group looked unsure about all this. She said 'When you say home care do you mean the care given in homes like residential homes?' 'No,' I replied chest slowly retracting, 'it's the care given to people in their own homes'. 'Oh,' she replied, 'you mean *home helps*'.

It was another lesson from the jar marked 'salutary'. I had lived with the phrase *'home care'* for so long and with *'domiciliary care'* (or *domcare* as it now seems to be known) entering the arena, I thought home care was the plain version. But there was an even plainer version. Some jargon is obvious to us. But some less so.

You will just have to be selective in your choice of words. Once again you must ask yourself 'will the audience understand this?' Let your answer decide whether you use it or not.

To be honest, I think you should avoid it as much as possible. Where you have to use it (for example *guardian ad litem*) simply take a sentence to explain what it means. Or better still explain what it is and then add 'this is known as a guardian ad litem' and so on.

You've been frameworked

Like all professions social services is only at peace with the world when it can relax to the gentle humming of its own buzz words. We carry out our work within a range of *frameworks*: legal, regulatory, anti-discriminatory, anti-oppressive and so on and on and on.

- *'Management Information Workshop - Framework for Discussion'.*
- *'The Registration and Inspection Unit operates within an agreed policy framework'.*
- *'A London Borough has produced a project manual for Best Value. The manual sets out six stages as a framework with back-up guidance materials on a range of issues including consultation with stakeholders'.*
- *'The Department of Health is currently developing a new framework for carrying out needs-led assessments of children and their families'.*
- *'The document also puts forward a common national framework so professionals can share information'.*

Robust jargon

As we approach the millennium, we know that our *services* should be seamless, needs-led and evidence-based. To meet these challenges we need to change (sorry, *refocus*) our strategies. We need to slip the word *robust* in somewhere. The relentlessly 'on-message' Junior Health Minister, Paul Boateng, was reported in the 16-22 October 1997 edition of *Community Care* as saying, in response to the Rikki Neave inquiry, that: 'Vital and robust measures are needed to protect children from the evil of abuse'. In the same issue, Sir Herbert Laming commenting on a Joint Review report on Sefton, said: 'Social services have little prospect of being restored unless the council's leadership takes robust and swift action'. I must, I must improve robust.

And finally...

Gross motor skills. I had no idea what this meant when I first came across it. I had always thought that the only people who had gross motor skills were the 17 year old boy or girl racers out in their XR2s. When I asked the person who wrote it what it meant, she told me it is the opposite to fine motor skills. Of course it is. All this motor stuff is driving me mad.

I can't handle trying to get to grips with *manipulative toys.* I'm entitled to not have to count on people lording it with their *peer relationships.* I feel dated by *chronological development.* I'm fed up with *specific dietary requirements.* And I don't think we should swallow it anymore.

Chapter 10

Gobbledygook

Gobbledygook

'This person was a deluge of words and a drizzle of thought'.

- *Peter de Vries* (from 'Comfort me with apples')

Gobbledygook (also spelt gobbledegook) was almost certainly coined to compare pretentious language with the incomprehensible gobble of a turkey cock. Maury Maverick, writing in the New York Times in 1944, defined gobbledygook as '...talk or writing which is long, pompous and vague, involved, usually with Latinized words...'

The word gobbledygook remained strictly an Americanism for years, with the stuffy British preferring their own 'officialese' (first recorded in 1884). However, it has become acceptable in modern English.

Gobbledygook is different from jargon. Jargon is a technical or specialist language but gobbledygook, to borrow Godfrey Howard's phrase, is writing 'that buries its meaning under polysyllabic incomprehensibility'. That is, using too many long words. It's language that nobody can understand. Quite often not even by the perpetrators of such stuff. Why say something simple and to the point when you can make it long winded and complicated? A gobbledygook-ish word that describes gobbledygook is obfuscation (from the Latin *obfuscatum*, which means 'to darken').

So a lie becomes a *terminological inexactitude*. The poor become the *economically marginalized*. A death in a hospital becomes *a negative patient outcome* - so, I guess, if you come out of a hospital alive you're classified as a *positive health outcome*. Staff stop knowing how to use computers and become *conversant with information technology*. The 'new management, new words' approach means that it is too painfully off-message and uncaring to take people and sack them, fire them or make them redundant. In these caring times, people are decruited, de-hired, outplaced, transitioned, rightsized, downsized, vocationally relocated or, rather deviously, offered a career-change opportunity. In essence, they have become surplus to the robust restructuring requirements outlined in the strategic plan.

In social services, we move seamlessly through analysing contra-indicators in our task-related work while employing negative re-enforcement responses. Job titles, it seems, were, how can I put it, linguistically impoverished. But not anymore. Everybody in social services is a manager of some sort. The prerequisite that managers needed to be responsible for people is long gone. Managers can now manage processes, projects and probably loads of other things beginning with p. Except as, experience tell us, a pastime that may well take place in a brewery.

Of course, it's not unique to social services. I remember when the senior in-flight customer services manager was the chief air steward(ess). As society becomes more tolerant it has quite rightly begun to examine its language. The quest for unisex language has seen air steward and stewardess crash land in favour of flight attendant. We're now taught that headmistress and headmaster should be headteacher. And *actress* has taken off the greasepaint for the last time as *actor* works for either male or female.

Social services departments have struggled to come up with terminology that appropriately describes the people they serve. Should they be known as users (drug links), clients (prostitution links... or rather sex-work links), customers (too M&S) or consumers (too commercial). May be the people we serve should be called just that - *people*. Or at least ask them what they would like to be known as.

I recall trying to out-liberal a social worker who was championing the term 'service user'. We were talking to a young man with Down's syndrome. I decided it was time to let the people decide. 'What would you prefer to be called,' I asked, adding helpfully 'you know, what would you *like* to be called?' The man looked at us both and said 'Colin'. Enough said.

Chapter 11

Being human

Being human

'Let us get away entirely from the chilly formalities of the old-style correspondence which seemed to come from some granite monolith rather than from another human being'.

*- an instruction from a President of the Board of Trade to his staff
(as quoted by Sir Ernest Gowers)*

There is a time and a place for formality. It just shouldn't be every time and every place. Most things that we write in social services do not need to be over-fed with stodgy helpings from a pan bubbling over with officialese. Remember that sometimes you are writing to people who are just like you. Before you send out a letter that you've written, think how you might feel if you had received it.

If you're replying to a letter, thank the person for theirs first. Most of the time you will want people to be on your side, to agree with you or to act on what you say. People will appreciate the fact that you've tried to address something personal to them and not just reeled off some badly photocopied standard letter.

Standard letters

Standard letters are usually ripe for rewrites. They have probably been used for years. No one ever reads them before signing them (if they even do that) because everyone knows what they say. Well, force yourself to read one. You may be surprised at how ugly, unfriendly and old fashioned it is. It might even remind you of your manager.

Example 1

The following is a standard reply sent out by a social services department acknowledging receipt of a complaint.

● *Representation and Complaints*

> *I wish to acknowledge receipt of your letter of * regarding your concerns. I am making further enquiries into this and will respond more fully to you as soon as I am in a position to do so.*
>
> *Yours sincerely*

First, the good points. At least they send out an acknowledgement. People understandably get upset if they don't hear anything, particularly if they have gone to the effort of putting down their concerns in writing. They will presume nothing is being done. The letter also uses the pronoun 'I' which gives the letter a welcome personal touch. This is better than using 'the department' or something equally faceless.

However, the language is cold and bureaucratic. It overuses stock phrases like '*acknowledge receipt of your letter*', '*making further enquiries*' and '*in a position to do so*'. Could '*in a position to do so*' mean once I am in a seating position at a desk? I'm sure it's not too difficult or too time consuming to have a more personal and relevant heading than 'Representation and Complaints'. Perhaps a warmer, more human letter might read:

● *Your complaint about home care*

> *Thank you for your letter dated *. I will be looking into your complaint and I will write to you again shortly.*
>
> *In the meantime, if there's anything else you would like to tell me, please feel free to contact me again.*
>
> *Yours sincerely*

What a difference a simple *'thank you'* makes. Even if someone is angry, a 'thank you' at the start of a letter can disarm people and make them feel you are looking after their interests. It is interesting how much easier something is to read if it makes use of *I, me, you, your, our* and so on. The reader gets a sense that something is being done and can contribute further to the process if they wish. It's also preferable to use the positive 'feel free' than the usual but negative 'do not hesitate to'.

Example 2

Here's an example of a letter sent out by an inspection unit.

- *Following the Post-registration Inspection of your home,
  Acid House, which took place on 7 February 1998, I
  enclose the report which has now been completed.*

  *As you know the report is, by law, to be made avail-
  able to the public and the report included here will be
  available to the public with effect from 7 April 1998.
  Please let me know before that date if there are any matters of a factual nature that you feel are incorrect and
  should be changed.*

On the positive side, the letter does use *I, me* and *you*. There's a *please*, which is welcome. The phrase *as you know* is a friendly sentence starter. However, you need to be careful as it can be used in a patronising or pompous way. Also, the phrase *by law*, although not strictly necessary to the overall message in this case, is preferable to the painfully over-worked *statutory requirement*.

However, the letter is rather long winded. I'm not convinced the phrase *Post-registration* is necessary in the first paragraph. Nor is the name of the home: I'm sure the owner or manager knows the name quite well. Even if the owner has hundreds of homes, the report's cover should tell them which part of their residential empire has come under scrutiny. Likewise the date of the inspection is surplus to requirements. As is the paragraph's last phrase *which has now been completed*: that much, at least, should be obvious.

The first sentence of the second paragraph is overlong and repetitive. Also, the over-official *matters of a factual nature* can become *mistakes*. A reworked letter could read as follows.

- *Please find enclosed the report on your recent inspection.
  As you know, all reports are now open to the public.
  This report will be available from 7 April 1998. Please let
  me know before then if you think there are any mistakes
  that you would like to change.*

Example 3

One final standard letter example is a notice of inspection sent out to the owner of a children's daycare service.

> ### NOTICE OF ANNUAL INSPECTION
>
> An appointment has been made to carry out the annual inspection of the premises known as St Ann's Playgroup at which you provide a daycare service.
>
> The inspection will take place on 15 March 1998. You are requested to complete the enclosed self-evaluation questionnaire and return it at least 14 days before your appointment.
>
> There is an annual fee payable for inspection of £10.00. This may be returned with the questionnaire or following the inspection, but must be paid within 28 days of the inspection date. Please ensure cheques are made payable to Wessex Council.

This letter is so mechanical I almost called out an engineer. The letter makes use of *you* and *your* but not *we* or *us*. The heading is in bold, capital letters and underlined, so it must be *really* important. This is overkill and can seem threatening to the reader.

There's no lead into the opening sentence: it's straight into your face. It's not a reply letter, so we can't plump for the *Thank you for your...* approach. I would suggest using the *We are writing to you...* approach. You could, of course, argue that it's an unnecessary phrase: it's obvious that we are writing to you because you've got the letter. But it is friendly, serves a purpose as a lead-in to a letter and it's harmless enough.

The last phrase *at which you provide a daycare service* is curious. You would think the owner might just have an inkling of what it is they do *at the premises known as St Ann's playgroup*. I can't imagine someone on receiving this letter staggering around their homes in bafflement, clutching their heads and repeatedly saying in escalating bemusement: 'What the hell do I do at St Ann's Church every morning of the week?'

The item enclosed with this letter may well be called a *self-evaluation questionnaire* but I think *form* does the job. And we more usually *fill in* forms rather than *complete* them. Also by asking for the return of the form at least 14 days before the inspection is a lazy request. It should be precise and give the date. The reader, who is already anxious because of the imminent inspection, now has to fret over working out how long they've got to fill a form in (or complete their self-evaluation questionnaire). You should try to make things easy for the reader.

The letter would also benefit from a friendlier tone. Even the '*You are requested...*' has a heavy handed feel to it. It could be replaced with '*Can we ask you...*' which is softer. Incidentally, although '*Can we ask you ...*' is a question, it doesn't take a question mark as it's not *asking* you it's actually *telling* you, albeit in a nice way.

A reworked version could read as follows.

Your annual inspection

*We are writing to inform you that we will be carrying out your annual inspection of St Ann's playgroup on **15 March 1998**.*

*Can we ask you to fill in the form we've enclosed and return it to us before **1 March 1998**.*

*There is an annual fee of £10 for your inspection. You can send this to us with the form if you wish. Or you can pay it after your inspection. However, please pay this fee by **12 April 1998**. Please make out your cheque to Wessex Council.*

Thank you.

With even local authorities finally getting to grips with new technology (my old department has just signed up Windows 74, I think) there is every reason to make standard letters more personal. Where one letter would stand in for every eventuality, you can now have as many different standard letters and forms as you need. For example, the inspection unit responsible for the above, could have five versions of the same letter. Each one could be personalised for full daycare nurseries, playgroups, crèches, holiday schemes and after school groups - all forms of registered daycare services for children but all different.

What it all means...

Being human means being polite in tone and conversational in style. It means saying please and thank you. It means letting the reader know that you're a real person not some faceless official. It means saying you're sorry if you should do so (pending legal advice and a full assessment by your council's insurers, obviously).

It means preferring a familiar phrase (*Thank you for your letter...*) to a cold, bureaucratic one (*Further to your correspondence last Thursday inst. 15 (iii) refers*). It means ending your letters with *Best wishes, Kind regards* or at least *Yours sincerely.* You should avoid *Yours faithfully, Yours very truly, I remain your obedient servant*, or anything like that. Unless, that is, you can remember the Somme or you're simply very sad. It means preferring pronouns (I, we, you). And it means using contractions (I'm, we're, you're, haven't). Just don't say you can't.

Chapter 12

A matter of style

A matter of style

'People think that I can teach them style. What stuff it all is!
Have something to say, and say it as clearly as you can.
That is the only secret of style'.

- *Matthew Arnold*

It is surprising just how many things in English are a matter for your - or somebody else's - preferred style. Tradition and convention have a say but it's your vote that counts. Here's a brief collection of items selected from social services writing.

/

The oblique line / is often used to represent *and/or*. It's a clumsy shorthand that has become compulsory in social services whether you mean *and/or*, or just *and*, and just *or*. It is preferable to write out in full what you mean. '*Parents and carers are encouraged to phone before visiting*'. '*Consent forms should be signed by a parent or guardian*'. '*The home can contact the external manager or the duty manager or both*'. A bit laborious but at least you will be clear.

Being positive

So, are you a half-glass full or a half-glass empty type of person? Being positive is a sound policy. Are dairy products advertised as 95% fat-free or as having 5% fat? Say the good things first. Even if you are writing a letter which has no good news at all for the reader, you can always begin with a '*Thank you for your letter…*' or '*Thank you for coming in to see me, it was good to meet you…*' You can also lead up to bad news with an 'I'm very sorry, but …' This simple politeness does help to soften the blow.

You should choose words that have a 'positive' feel. Some words do carry a negative baggage and you can avoid words like *should not* by using a word such as, well, *avoid*. I realise that this advice is contradictory to the style of this book that makes great use of words like *can't, shouldn't* and *won't*. But they are employed lightly, in keeping with the spirit of the book and don't set out to club you round the head.

You can try to make the negative sound more positive. For example, I remember a children's home having a rule that 'children cannot go out after midnight'. I suggested they change the rule to read that 'children should be in by midnight'. It says the same thing, only positively. I've noticed many local authorities employ this tactic for their complaints procedures. They welcome comments on what they do well and on *what can be improved* rather than what they do not do well. Here are some examples of negative writing put more positively.

Children are not left unsupervised.

Children are always supervised.

Do windows or glass doors present a safety hazard?

Are windows and glass doors safe?

Staff spoke of their intention to discourage dependency in residents.

Staff said they intended to encourage residents to be independent.

Though there are a number of outstanding maintenance issues requiring attention, the building is in a good state of repair.

The building is in a good state of repair. However, there are some repairs that need to be done.

Being specific

Prefer the precise to the vague. You might live in your domestic resource facility. I live in my home. This means preferring *Nursery Inspection Report* to: *Registration of Day Care Provision Inspection Report.*

It means that people might have a *lockable chest of drawers* rather than a *lockable piece of furniture*. It means that rather than writing 'the registration certificate was displayed in a conspicuous place', you say where that place was.

Capital letters

Keep these to a minimum. Start a sentence with them, give them to names of people, titles and places. And after those keep away from the *caps lock* or *shift* keys. Capital letters in the middle of text can look ugly if overused. Lines of capital letters are unread-able. This is because there is no shape to capital letters, they hit you in blocks. Lower case letters go up down flying around. That makes them more readable. AND MORE FRIENDLY TO LOOK AT AS THEY DON'T SHOUT AT YOU. Think of how many road signs you see written out in full capital letters. Lower case is easier and quicker to read.

You should also be prudent in their use. Sometimes their use is less than democratic. All too often we give capital letters to The Home's Managers, Officers or Keyworkers but don't for the cook, domestic staff and carers. Either give them all capital letters or (preferably) none of them. It can seem pompous, as in these examples: *The Inspector and lay assessor feel positive about care practice.* The Inspector is obviously more important than a meagre forelock tugging lower case lay assessor. *The Management and staff appear clear about what they are aiming to achieve.* The simple guide is *be consistent.*

Flesch formula

Sometimes called the Flesch readability formula, this influential technique claims to test the ease with which a text is read. It is named after an American Rudolf Flesch who developed the text in his book *The Art of Readable Writing* in 1949. To work out your score manually (a number of wordprocessing packages will do it automatically for you) you need to:

- count the number of words you have used (say 205)
- count the number of syllables (say 299)
- count the number of sentences (say 17)
- divide the number of syllables (299) by the number of words (205) - which gives us the average word length (1.46)

- divide the number of words (205) by the number of sentences (17) - which gives us the average sentence length (12.1)

- multiply the average word length (1.46) by 84.6 (=123.52)

- multiply the average sentence length (12.1) by 1.015 (= 12.28)

- add together the above two answers (123.52+ 12.28 = 135.8)

- subtract this number (135.8) from 206.835 (= 71.04)

- this is your readability score.

The reading ease scale runs from 0 (unreadable) to 100 (easy to read). Plain English is said to be around a score of 60.

This entry on the Flesch formula scored 81.1. The whole book scored 68.7.

In the United States a number of states insist that things like insurance documents score between 50 and 60 on the Flesch formula. Indeed, in 1978 President Jimmy Carter passed Executive Order No. 12044 that required all state laws and regulations to be written in plain English. Interestingly, this was revoked in 1981 by Executive Order No. 12291 passed by President Ronald Reagan.

You shouldn't take this type of test (others include the Fog index) too seriously but it is a useful guide. And anything that binds us to more readable words is okay in my book.

Grammar checkers

These are programmes on computers that check your grammar for you. But you should only use them if one or more of the following apply: you are a sad traditionalist; you are living in another age; you are frankly appalled at what people like me say about language. If not, they are best avoided as the people who write these programmes are to creative understanding what King Herod was to childminding. These are people who think four foot long spreadsheets are things of beauty. Beware grammar checkers unless you can be sure there is an 'ignore rule' command.

Headings

With computers, wordprocessing and the like, I am still amazed that people overload headings with capital letters, emboldened print and underlining. Really, one of them will do. Using bold letters is effective on its own. Too many capital letters are hard to read and they can come across as threatening. Underlining words is ugly, distracting and difficult to read. Apart from that, it's fine. You lose the clarity of your type if you use lower case as the line cuts through the tails of p, q, y, g, and j. For example:

<u>Application for Registration as Manager</u>

The following is over the top.

<u>MENUS, MEALS AND CATERING ARRANGEMENTS</u>

It really is enough to put:

Menus, meals and catering arrangements

Or if you want to add that little zest of extra emphasis, try a different typeface or try the next font size up:

Menus, meals and catering arrangements

You'll never go back to your old washing powder again. Actually, the example could be easily replaced with:

Food

But I am a simple man. Finally, headings are useful at the top of letters. This allows the reader to know the subject matter straight-away. However, if you are one of the 99.5% of social services people who start a heading with *Re:-*, please ask yourself why you do this.

Re:- "The Children Act" 1989

You could rework this example without the *'Re:-'*, the messy punctuation and without the incorrect title of the Act.

Children Act 1989

The *Re:-* adds nothing. Kill it off. And send no flowers.

Inspector as estate agent

When describing homes it's hard for inspectors not to slip into estate agent speak. *The main dining room and communal sitting areas are pleasant and tastefully appointed. The home is in good decorative order throughout.* No doubt the weekly fee to live in these homes includes all carpets and curtains.

Lists

Lists are good ways to break up information and can help your page look good. However, three things to remember about lists are that:-

- you don't need to use :- to introduce one, a simple colon (:) does the job;
- You should be consistent, starting each item with lower case or upper case letters but never mixing them up together, unlike this example; *and*
- that each new item has to follow on from the introduction to the list to make a completed sentence that makes sense, unlike this example.

N/A

Beloved of form fillers the world over. This abbreviation for 'not applicable' is perhaps too widespread to campaign for its demise. If you had to write it out in full, you probably wouldn't use *applicable.*

You might prefer *relevant.* Maybe we should write N/R. The general guide is to avoid abbreviations.

NB, nb

NB or *nb* are abbreviations for nota bene, which is Latin for 'note' or 'mark well'. As it's Latin, I shall be consistent and advise you to junk it. Prefer *Please note.*

Numbers

You shouldn't start a sentence with a number in figures. Always write them out in full. *3 rooms are used by nursery children.* This looks ungainly. So prefer: *Three rooms are used by nursery children.* There are no strict rules about how you use numbers in your text but you should be consistent. If you are cast adrift in the hopelessness of it all, and seek guidance - here's some: numbers up to ten should be written out in full, all others can be figures. *Sixteen children and 2 staff members were present* simply looks better as *Sixteen children and two staff members were present.* However, you should use numbers as figures when that helps understanding. This example is confusing: *'4 new care staff are undertaking NVQ level 2 and 1 is doing level 3'.* If you keep the staff numbers written in full and the NVQ levels as figures, the meaning is clearer. *'Four new care staff are undertaking NVQ level 2, and one is doing level 3'.* Also avoid mixing up written numbers and figures as in this example: *'There is Public Liability Insurance of 1 and a half million'.*

'phone

I still see this from time to time. The apostrophe indicating that some of the word is missing (tele). However, phone is well established as a word in its own right. So, disconnect the apostrophe. I've even come across 'bus. I don't know many people who even remember that the word in full is *omnibus,* so it might even confuse people or cause them to think there's been a typing error.

We can't carry passengers, so give the apostrophe a one way ticket out of town.

Order of things

I know that in these democratic times we should view all things equally, but that's not the case when it comes to lists. People will think that whatever comes first in a list is the most important and what comes last is least important. And they will stubbornly think this is the case even if you put in an 'in no particular order' disclaimer. The following is from an inspection report. '*The views of the proprietors, night and day workers and residents were sought*'. Perhaps residents are down the list of important people to talk to for some inspectors. If that's the case may be it's time to hang up their clipboards (they probably have them to hang up, as well). Residents are clearly the most important people, so put them up front.

Political correctness

Not so much a label as an insult, so-called political correctness (PC) has had and is having a tough time. And on those occasions when it is taken to an extreme, perhaps deservedly so. However, we should not underestimate the power of words and language. And words, at times, will have meanings that are inappropriate or offensive. Sometimes this will be implicit, sometimes explicit. We should have a duty of care with the words we choose. We should be sensitive to the wishes and feelings of those who read what we write. However, sensitivity is one thing, paranoia quite another.

It was understandable why the Spastics Society became Scope. The word *spastic* has taken on a popular impoliteness that makes it awkward and embarrassing to use in its original sense. Similarly, it was understandable to change the label for *mental handicap*, because the word '*mental*' has come to mean *mad* or *crazy*. Also, the word 'handicapped' has had its day and was generally felt to be too negative. PC (or '*appropriately inclusive*') alternatives for mental handicap were *learning disabilities* or *learning difficulties* depending on your department's preference. I'm still awaiting the day that Mencap relaunch themselves as Learndis or Learndiff, depending on their preference. The only preference we don't seem to take into account is that of the people we seek so desperately to label.

However, the extreme of calling older people *experientially enhanced* is farcical and unnecessary. It only serves to whet the egos of those who come up with such absurdities and does sensitivity and understanding a dis-service. As does opposing such words as *manufacture* and *manager* on the grounds that they both start with 'man' and are therefore linguist symbols of patriarchal oppression. However, the derivation of these words come from the Latin *manus,* which means 'hand'. On the other hand, we should clearly avoid phrases like man-made, workman and man-hours. PC has had a bad press, which to a healthy cynic like me means that it must be good. Language is powerful and it does affect and reflect the way we live. As such there is a need for language to reflect and promote the equality of a society that we should all want to live in. The simple reason why we should think carefully about our use of language is because we really should have a respect for others. And I think at the heart of PC is *respect.* We should respect the feelings of others as best we can.

pp, p.p.

More Latin. This stands for 'per procurationem' meaning 'by proxy' or 'on behalf of'. If someone has to sign things on your behalf, then use 'for'. Anyone still using 'for and on behalf of' is indulging in unnecessary legalese and should take the appropriate medication immediately.

References

References (2.1, 7.5) are useful in long documents, particularly those sent out for consultation or comment. Again, think about who's going to read your document. A technical document for other technicians will probably function adequately with complex referencing. However, there are one or two points to bear in mind. Remember references are supposed to be just that - a point of reference, so keep your numbering simple. It's a good guide to try to keep to one decimal place (4.6). However, there's a tendency in social services writing to go to a minimum of two places (2.1.4). Two places have to be your maximum. If you really need to number more than one decimal place consider using bullet points. You should certainly avoid things like the following which was part of a complaints procedure document for staff: *'Please refer to Section 6.4.1 3(c) in Appendix II'*. I once read an inspection report that listed the action taken on previous recommendations. There were 88 of them. The report numbered them in roman numerals. While I was impressed that the writer knew what 88 was in roman numerals (LXXXVIII), it had ceased to become a reference point for anybody except Caligula. And maybe his horse. Something else to avoid is the computer geek's preference for numbering a section *2.0*. It is plain, all right. Plain silly. Finally, when referencing, stick to numbers: they're the most easily understood. Avoid letters (A2, 6c) and lower case roman numerals (i, ii, iii).

Times of day

Normally I'm happy to move with the times. But not this time. Avoid the twenty four hour clock. Really, I'm not winding you up.

'The inspection took place between 16.00 hours and 19.30 hours'.

Not for me, it didn't. It took place between 4pm and 7.30pm.

Unisex grammar

There will be times for reasons of confidentiality, convenience or otherwise that you feel the need to resort to *he/she, s/he, her/him, (s)he*. The only way to avoid these messy constructions is to use plurals (*them, they, their*) and use them in a singular sense. So instead of *The resident went to his/her room*, you can have *The resident went to their room.* The logical extension to this is *themself.* This causes people to run home and bolt the doors. I believe it's useful: *The client then made themself something to eat.* It's not generally accepted but I think we're getting there. There may not be light at the end of the tunnel yet, but we can certainly see the tunnel.

Unisex words

There are some places (still) that prefer male dominated language. I know at least one council where the Chair*man* of Social Services Committee is a woman. Others have Chairwomen, but most now prefer to call themselves after a piece of furniture: Chair. The only real guide around all this is to ask the person performing the duty what title *they* would prefer.

Chapter 13

Good by design

Good by design

'It is to be noted that when any part of this paper appears dull there is a design in it'.

- Sir Richard Steele

The content is always going to be the most important feature of anything you write. But don't underestimate the power of what your letter, report or memo looks like. A clear layout of your work can attract people to what you have to say and help with clarity. On the other hand, a very poor layout may result in people filing your work under '*bin*' unread.

Your organisation may have a defined *house style* that you are expected to follow. That's fine. It's good that your organisation has thought about this. However, depending on your target audience there might be grounds for challenging the appropriateness of your house style.

While I was Head of Inspection at Barking & Dagenham, I deliberately sought to produce information in different ways to the corporate and departmental styles. The formal reason I gave hinged on the need to promote the so-called arm's length independence of the inspection unit. However, the real reason was that I didn't like the formality or dullness of the preferred style.

You don't need a diploma in Design to produce work that looks good. Graphics and illustrations are welcome but aren't always easily available to people. However, there are some things you can try if you have a computer to help you.

Before you decide what a document should look like, think of yourself as a reader rather than a writer. Think about the things that attract and irritate you. If you make a list of each of these you will probably find that the work your department produces is more likely to meet the criteria of what irritates you than what attracts you. This is because we don't think enough (or at all) about design. Here are some basic tips.

Covers

Covers are particularly important for longer reports. A good cover can give a report a professional edge. If you can and the report warrants it, use card or thicker paper than the rest of the report for your cover. Inspection reports which are available to the public benefit greatly from distinctive covers. A cover should have all the information needed to identify the report.

You should at least have a title page. The cover should leave the reader clear about what goes on behind it. Only use essential information as too much detail or too much text on the cover can be off-putting.

Layout

Longer reports will benefit from using all or some of the following sections as appropriate.

- Contents
- Summary
- Introduction
- Summary of recommendations
- Main findings
- Report
- Conclusion

It is helpful to have a summary at the beginning. This allows the reader to find out what the report is about and take a decision whether or not they need to read the full report. Sometimes summaries come at the end of a report. But this seems illogical as you will be reading a summary after you've read the full report. By that time you don't need it.

Some people will argue that the contents page will tell you where to find the summary. But this simply makes life difficult for the reader. The reader will pick up the report and will decide how important the subject is dependent on the title page or cover. If interested the reader will then turn the page to see the summary. If still interested, the reader will then move on through the document. Your report will be competing with others, and people need to be selective about what they read. The advised headings help people with that process. People will stop you in supermarkets and thank you for your help.

Think 'space'

The more space you have on your page, the easier it will be to read. If you are confronted with huge tracts of unrelenting text, it feels too much like hard work to plough through it all. And yet you put the same amount of text over two pages, although using more paper, can feel shorter. It can seem more manageable.

Thinking 'space' means using margins on both sides of paper; giving headings room to breathe and not suffocating them with text above and below; using lists, bullet points, charts and boxes to help break up text; starting sections on new pages, even if this means leaving space at the bottom of the page.

Typed reports will benefit from being single-sided rather than double-sided. This means that when a page is turned, a blank sheet will accompany a typed sheet. Once again the effect is to make the text appear more manageable. If confronted with two full pages of text it may panic the reader who feels there is just too much to get through. The less committed reader will then either skim or give up.

The use of space, while aiding readability can also seem wasteful. As rainforests disappear and Sting becomes more agitated, we should be sensible. Some authorities have a policy to use both sides of paper in a laudable attempt to save paper. If yours is one, then you should follow this policy. However, it's also worth remembering that if nobody reads what you produce then all you have been doing is wasting your time. And time, like paper, is an important resource that needs to be managed.

Typeface and font

A typeface is the shape and design of letters or type. This is Univers.
A typeface is the shape and design of letters or type. This is CG Times.
A typeface is the shape and design of letters or type. This is Times New Roman.
A typeface is the shape and design of letters or type. This is Garamond.

You can see from these examples that each typeface has different widths and some look bigger than others. Univers looks bigger because the 'small' letters like i, a, n, x, are proportionately bigger to the larger letters like f, h, k and so on.

It's important when selecting a typeface you use one that is clean, clear and easy to read. And one that keeps these characteristics even after being sentenced to hours of hard labour in photocopier hell. Too often when realising that there are so many typeface designs to choose from, people go for elaborate ones that they think look impressive. These typefaces usually have lots of serifs - that's curly bits to you and me. They might be pretty but usually they are hard to read and should be left to wedding invitations and the like.

Font is the size of the print you use. It is measured in *points*. A point is about 1/72 of an inch. You shouldn't drop below 10 point but 12 point is advisable. Although you will need to try out different fonts as some typefaces seem small even at 12 point. Again, remembering your target audience, you should use larger print for people who may have difficulty reading small print.

Portrait or landscape

These terms refer to which way round your paper is. Both of them relate to painting. A portrait picture would have a shorter width than length. And to talk the technical talk: a landscape picture would be longer across the top than down the sides.

Portrait is the more conventional of the two. People (or at least right-handed people) find it easier turning pages from right to left than from bottom to top. Reports that are written using landscape are awkward to read. It is also annoying to have to keep swapping a report around if the writer has made use of both portrait and landscape. Landscape is often preferred by people who draw charts. These people probably work in your organisation's IT department. Or are overused and overpaid management consultants who use landscape with an alarming regularity in attempts to justify their bloated invoices. They think landscape looks impressive. It doesn't. There are, of course, times when a particular and essential chart or graph simply doesn't fit comfortably into portrait. In these cases, landscape is the unavoidable answer. However, on the face of it - prefer portrait.

Highlighting text

There are a number of ways to highlight text. **You can put it in bold.** *You can put it in italic.* <u>You can (if you have to) underline it but this can look clumsy</u>, and certainly not recommended by this book. You can use larger fonts, particularly for headings. You can use lists, bullet points, charts and boxes. Apart from underlining words, although I do use lines, this book makes use of all these devices. Sometimes, **but sparingly,** combining two of them.

Indeed using bold and italics consistently can help improve clarity. The following example is drawn from an inspection report that adopted a question-answer approach. The layout is confusing.

Is there a personal file on each staff member?   YES
Do the files contain the following:-

There is one at the nursery and one at Company head office.
An application form?

There is on all staff appointed since the new Person in
Charge has been appointed.

Details of previous employment?   YES

Where application forms are in the nursery.

The use of space has complicated things. The YES answers are stranded across the page away from the question. The example has not been helped by an out of sequence comment to the first question. The following is an example of how it might look.

Is there a personal file on each staff member? **YES**
There is one at the nursery and one at Company head office.

Do the files contain the following:
• An application form? **YES**
There is on all staff appointed since the new Person in Charge has been appointed.

- Details of previous employment? **YES**
Where application forms are in the nursery.

It is now clear that the italicised text is a comment on the question. Better use has been made of space as its now clear which comment relates to each question. It is a good example of how design can help improve clarity.

Chapter 14

Dos, don'ts and maybes*

*apologies to Bernstein, but it is such a cool phrase

Fig.1 FLAMMABLE SOFA

Fig.2 INFLAMMABLE SOFA

Dos, don'ts and maybes

**'If language is not correct, then what is said is not what is meant;
if what is said is not what is meant,
then what ought to be done remains undone'.**

- Confucious

English is full of words that cause more trouble than they're worth. This chapter looks briefly at some words which I've come across in social services writing that have been misused.

advice, advise

Commonly misused. As in *'This is in keeping with the advise of the Community pharmacist'*. Advice is the noun (*to give and take advice*) while advise is the verb (*'I must advise you to read all the reports I've given you'*).

We seem to spend an inordinate amount of time advising people (*'The inspector was advised that emergency admissions do not take place at the Home...'* *'Members are advised that the next Committee will receive a full report on this issue')* when we really should be plain old **informing** them. You are only offering advice if there is an element of choice involved and you are suggesting an option

affect, effect

It's not unusual to see these two words mixed up, as in the following example. *'Have there been any changes to the external premises that effect their suitability for childminding?'*

The verb ***affect*** means to influence: *'the aim of this book is to affect the way you write in the future'*.

The verb ***effect*** means to bring about: *'the team felt they could effect some changes in the way they worked'*.

The noun **effect** means consequence: *'the book had an effect on the team'.*

agenda

There will no doubt be people in your department who will claim, their words dripping in smugness, that actually it's not agenda, it should be *agendum*. 'Agenda is plural' they will say. But only in Latin. It's now a fully fledged English word. And in English it's singular. Therefore, the plural is 'agendas'. And you should minute that. Ditto data and datum.

all right

There is an occasional tendency to write *alright* instead of *all right*. These two words are ripe for becoming one. But at the moment they most definitely are not. So use two. All right?

ancillary

Often applied to non-care staff, this word has little to commend it. It's based on a word that means *handmaiden*. Ancillary is defined in the *Shorter Oxford English Dictionary* as *subservient, subordinate*. Prefer *support staff* or *other staff*.

anticipate

This means *to pre-empt* (plan and prepare for something) and not *to expect*. However, it is used so often to mean expect that I fully anticipate it's only a matter of time before it does.

blueprint

A term from the whacky world of engineering. If you *have* to use it, use it to mean the final plan and not draft or outline. As any engineer worth his set square will tell you: the blueprint is the final design off the drawing board.

can, may

Can means that something is possible. For example, you can turn up three hours late for work every day. *May* carries a sense of permission: you *can* turn up three hours late for work every day, but you *may* not.

complement, compliment

A common mistake. If something *complements* another thing, it adds to it. If you *compliment* someone you are praising them for something. This example from an inspection report not only highlights an old-fashioned use of the word *complement* but also spells it incorrectly: *'The home's staff compliment is as follows:-'*.

criterion, criteria

There is only one *criterion*, but there are at least two *criteria*.

discrete, discreet

There's lots of talk in social services about *discrete* areas of work. This means a separate or particular area of work. If those who use it refuse to use a plainer alternative, they should at least spell it properly. *Discreet* means being careful and avoiding embarrassment. Or maybe that's what they meant after all.

first, firstly

Strangely this has excited huge debate. As far as we are concerned, either is fine. *Firstly, secondly,* and so on are as acceptable as *first, second,* and so on. *Firstly,* who really cares and, *second* just be more consistent than me.

flammable, inflammable

Such is the English language that inflammable actually means flammable. Prefer *non-flammable*.

include

When you use *include* you only need to list a selection of the things that form the whole. For example: *the council's depart-*

ments include Social Services, Housing and Leisure Services. You don't need to list them all. Also the use of *'and so on'* at the end of your list is unnecessary as the word *include* already tells us that the list is not complete.

needless to say

Then don't say it.

obviously

If it's obvious, why are you telling someone?

on, upon

Should it be *upon receipt of your report* or *on receipt of your report*? There's no distinction between *on* or *upon*. Whichever you use is yours by choice.

openness

Always with two *n*s, openness is something that social services senior management teams claim to be all about. The buzz phrase is openness and honesty. However, most of them are about as open as my local at 2am (to me, anyway) and about as honest as the day is short.

per se

A Latin term for *'in itself'*, *'essentially'* or *'as such'*. As with most Latin terms there are alternative, plainer English words. *Per se* can be left out as it usually adds nothing to a sentence. But if you need to make the point - use English words.

principle, principal

Another twin set of troublesome words. Principle is always a noun and is a rule or standard: *'The Home is sticking to its principles'*. Principal can be a noun (Principal Officer) or a descriptive word (adjective) meaning main. *'The principal reason for inspection is to protect vulnerable people'*.

that, which

There's a lot of fuss about this. But you don't need to add to it. If you really want to distinguish between the two: use *that* when it's essential to the meaning; and use *which* when it is providing incidental information. *'The Review decided that it was in the client's best interests to attend the centre'*. But: *'The Review, which was the second one this year, decided it was in the client's best interests to attend the centre'*.

vice-versa

More Latin, more words to avoid. It means literally 'the position having been turned'. Prefer the English alternative: *the other way round.*

wear and tear

This is an excellent plain phrase when spoken. However, written down it causes problems. Or in social work terms, it *presents challenges*. It looks odd and people may have difficulty in deciding how to read it. If it was spelt ware and tare, there would be no ...em...challenge presented.

Chapter 15

Putting it all together

Putting it all together

'I notice that you use plain, simple language, short words and brief sentences. That is the way to write English. It is the modern way and the best way. Stick to it'.

- Mark Twain

This chapter has nothing to say. It's all show. Other chapters have made use of examples to show specific elements of plain English. This last chapter uses five examples to brings all those elements together.

■ Example 1

These inspections have been undertaken as part of the bi-annual inspection that is a requirement under the N.H.S and Community Care Act 1990.

- *Bi-annual* is often misinterpreted as every two (bi-ennial) years rather than twice a year. So, to avoid confusion, spell it out.
- *Undertaken* can be replaced by *carried out* or rather *carry out*, if we prefer a more active approach.
- Giving the Act its full title is perhaps unnecessary.
- The statement can also be made more human by adding a *we*.

It could be rewritten as:
- *By law, we carry out these inspections twice a year.*

■ Example 2

There are tea making facilities should any resident wish to avail themselves. Not all are acceptable but some do take advantage.

This has little to commend it. You could interpret the second sentence to be saying that the residents themselves are not acceptable (who to? the inspector?) rather than whether they choose to use the facilities or not. Or it could mean that the tea making equipment was not good enough.

- *avail* is pompous. Prefer *use*.
- *acceptable* is the wrong word for 'choose to'. It is also pompous and unnecessary as the second part of the sentence says the same thing.
- residents *taking advantage* is an unfortunate phrase as it implies abuse.
- in essence what's being said is that there are tea making facilities and some residents use it, some don't. I think that the phrase *tea making facilities* has been brewing for some time and is quite well understood. Although, this is largely thanks to Britain's bed and breakfast traders and hoteliers who regularly offer this as standard. However, you could argue that in this example it is not really adding anything because if residents make themselves a drink they must have used the facilities. The probable point being made is that it's a hot drink (tea, coffee, whatever) that they're making.

It could be rewritten as:
- *Some residents make themselves a hot drink*

▌ Example 3

> *NB   "Any person wishing to publish this report or make extracts from it, is required to seek written permission from the Registration Authority prior to publication".*

This sentiment is common for inspection units that have had experience of homes that publicise themselves by 'quoting' selective passages from reports that may otherwise be damning. It has a legal flavouring. This is scary as the only people who think that solicitors and lawyers write well are the solicitors and lawyers themselves.

- note this well: try and avoid using *NB* or *nb*. The English *Please note* is easier to understand, more polite and infinitely preferable.
- the whole piece is impersonal - *any person* rather than *you*, for example. Actually the phrase *any person rather than you* reminds me of the outcome of most of my night club flirtations. Still, that's another book. Or leaflet. Or post-it note. Or stamp.
- replace *extracts* with *parts of*
- *required to seek* is pompous. Prefer *must have*
- *prior to publication* is pompous and ambiguous: is it before the report is published by the Registration Authority or before *the person* publishes their preferred *extract?*
- there is no follow up information - who do I contact, where, when, how?

It could be rewritten as:

- ***Please note.** If you want to publish this report in full or parts of it, you must first have written permission from us. Please ring Darren Huckerby on ** for more information.*

▌ Example 4

Management should reassess its recruitment procedures in order to increase the number of care staff with residential experience.

....

This is just a slightly pompous way of saying:

- *Management should look to recruit more staff with experience of working in a care home.*

▌ Example 5

Inspectors suggested that consideration be given to radical re-design of the grounds which are extensive and grossly underused.

....

There are a number of words used here that have plainer alternatives:

- *consideration* could be replaced with *thought*. But in this case it can be left out.
- *radical re-design* is a shockingly excitable phrase that basically means that the gardens need work on them: a calmer and plainer alternative.
- *extensive* can be replaced with *large*.
- *grossly* is grossly out of place.

It could be rewritten as:

- *Inspectors suggested that work should be done on the large grounds as not much use is made of them at the moment.*

Chapter 16

Conclusion

Conclusion

'Sir, 'tis my occupation to be plain'.

- *William Shakespeare* (King Lear)

Investing time now

As a stuffy room needs a window opened occasionally, so stuffy writing needs a breath of fresh air. In writing for the public, I believe plain English is that breath of fresh air.

When it comes to your writing only you can open that window. And admitting to yourself that you need it open is the first (very big) step you need to take. Once you have done, the hard work begins. It's unlikely that you will be able to switch between writing styles with the greatest of ease.

It will take you time to get to grips with plain English. Things that you could knock out in minutes will start taking three, four, five times as long. But if you resist the temptation to slip back into the old habits - which will for some time seem more snug and comfortable than the irritable, uneasy fit of plain English - fluency, speed and understanding will come. It will seem a bit like reluctantly giving up your old shoes for a new pair. And once you've dug your heels in, you'll have to start imagining your-self in the shoes of the people you are writing for. After reading this book, perhaps a few Saturdays in Freeman, Hardy & Willis will help you make sense of it all.

Accuracy

This book has concerned itself with not *what* you write but rather *how* you write it. I've spoken about things like the Flesch formula and Fog index that analyse the readability of your written work. However, these only care about whether or not what you have to say can be under-stood. They don't take into account the quality of your arguments or the relevance or importance of what you are trying to say. They don't take into account the accuracy or legitimacy of what you have to say. It's important that in fostering the principles of plain English we also adopt the principles of accuracy, clarity of purpose and honesty. For without these all else is worthless. And the work we do and the people we serve are anything but.

Your next steps

So, apart from taking your guide from this book, what else can you do? How will you know whether you are truly producing written information that is easily understood?

Well, there are at least three things you can do: set up guidelines for staff; seek outside approval; and set up groups of local people.

Guidelines for staff

This means writing a manual of house style. If your council or organisation are resistant, think smaller: think departmental. No joy, think divisional. No joy, think section or team. From small acorns…

If you feel restricted by time or experience to do this yourself or with colleagues, think about bringing somebody in from outside. Actually, I'm very reasonable. However, my fees are not.

Outside approval

This can be expensive. So tell your mangers that 'it's external validation that can benchmark our public communication strategy in line with Best Value'. They'll fall for it. Wholesale.

I'm only aware of two organisations that provide this service: *Plain English Campaign* (who analyse, edit and award crystal marks for approved written information) and *The Word Centre* (who do much the same).

Set up groups of local people

This is the hardest to organise. But is probably the cheapest in terms of hard currency being spent and definitely the richest in terms of relevance and feedback. If you think you will never be allowed to get away with doing this, impress your managers by calling it a New Labour-inspired *focus group*.

Back in 1993, in Barking & Dagenham, I set up what we agreed to call a lay readers panel. I worked in partnership with a local comprehensive school who were running a Health and Social Care class for sixth form pupils. Every major piece of publicity would be vetted by the pupils on this panel. If they understood it, we printed it. We toyed with the idea of awarding publicity that was passed a 'Well Crystal' mark but thought better of it.

Ever since I started work in the inspection unit in 1991, I have tried to include members of the public in our work - through consultation, on our advisory groups and on inspections. These people always received a draft copy of everything the unit was looking to publish, including standards, leaflets, newsletters, posters, reports and job advertisements. If local people approve and understand the things you are to publish, then what greater approval could you wish for?

Concluding the conclusion

I've carried out training courses on plain English for local authorities since 1996. Each training day has ended with the same quote. I intend to end this book in the same way. It's a quote that comes from '*Plain Words - A guide to the use of English*' by Sir Ernest Gowers. Gowers was invited by the Treasury to write a guidance book for the use of English by civil servants writing to and for the public. It was published originally in 1948. Over fifty years later, it still says it all for me. His advice was: **'Be short. Be simple. Be human'**.

And if you remember and take this advice when you are writing with the public in mind then the chances are that they will understand you. And that they will be able to make their own minds up about what you're saying. And I don't mind that. Not a bit of it.

Sources

Aitchison, James (1994). *Cassell Guide to Written English*. London.

Bryson, Bill (1990). *Mother Tongue*. London.

Bryson, Bill (1987). *Troublesome Words*. London.

Burchfield, RW, (ed.) (1996). *The New Fowler's Modern English Usage*. Oxford.

Chambers Dictionary of Foreign Words and Phrases. (1995). Edinburgh.

Cohen, JM and MJ (1973). *A Dictionary of Modern Quotations*. London.

Collins Plain English Dictionary. (1996). London

Collinson, Diane, (et al.) (1993). *Plain English*. Buckingham.

Community Care, weekly magazine

Crystal, David (1988). *The English Language*. London.

Crystal, David (1992) *The Cambridge Encyclopedia of Language*. Cambridge.

Cutts, Martin (1996). *The Plain English Guide*. Oxford.

Doyle, Margaret (1995). *The A-Z of Non-Sexist Language*. London.

Dunant, Sarah, (ed.) (1995). *The War of the Words*. London.

Gowers, Ernest (1951). *ABC of Plain Words*. London.

Gowers, Ernest (1948). *Plain Words*. London.

Gowers, Ernest (1954) *The Complete Plain Words*. London.

Howard, Godfrey (1993). *The Good English Guide*. London.

Jenkins, Simon, (ed.) (1992). *English Style and Usage*. London.

Jespersen, Otto (1993) *Essentials of English Grammar*. London.

Marshall, Jeremy and McDonald, Fred (1994). *Questions of English*. Oxford.

McArthur, Tom, (ed.) (1992). *Oxford Companion to the English Language*. Oxford.

Oxford Dictionary of English Etymology. (1993). Oxford.

Oxford Dictionary of English Grammar. (1994). Oxford.

Oxford Dictionary of Quotations. (1990). Oxford.

Oxford English. (1986). Oxford.

Oxford Guide to English Usage. (1994). Oxford.

Partridge, Eric (1981). *Usage and Abusage*. London.

Roget's Thesaurus. (1981). London.

Shorter Oxford English Dictionary. (1983). Oxford.

Tucker, Susie I, (ed.) (1974). *English Examined*. Connecticut.

Venolia, Jan (1991). *Write Right!*. Nairn.

...and all those who sent in their work as part of plain English training courses between 1996 and 1998.

Index

abbreviation 22, 68, 101-102
abstract words 9, 11, 45
accuracy 128
acronym 17, 76
active voice (or verb) 45-47
adjectives 9
adverbs 9-10
apostrophe 10, 21-23, 29, 103

basis 35, 41-42
being human 87-94
being positive 96-97
brackets 24, 25
buzzwords 53, 80

capital letters 79, 91, 98, 100
Clarity 77
clause 7, 10, 45, 62
colon 16, 19-20, 65, 101
comma 11, 16-19, 24-25, 31,
    65-66, 68
computer 74-76, 84, 99
concrete words 9
conjunction 10, 66
contraction 10, 22, 93
cover 90, 109

editing 34, 37
ellipsis (dots) 25
exclamation marks 20-21, 62

Flesch formula 98-99, 128
full stop 16-17, 20, 62, 65-66

gobbledygook 83-86
grammar 5-14, 47
grammar checker 99-100
grammar, unisex 105-106

headings 100-101, 110, 112
health service 78
highlighting text 112
hyphen 23-25

jargon 2, 4, 10, 20, 71-80, 84

landscape 111
Latin 7, 8, 11-12, 68, 77, 84,
    102, 104, 117, 119-120
layout 108-109
lazy writing 30-31
lists 20, 69, 101

nouns 9, 12-13, 22
numbers 17, 102, 104-105

padding 39-50
passive voice (or verb) 47-49
Plain English Campaign 76, 78,
    129
point of reference 104-105
political correctness 103-104
portrait 111
preposition 12-13
prescriptive grammar 7-8
punctuation 15-27, 101

question marks 20-21, 62, 92

semi colons 19-20
sentence 10, 12, 16, 18, 102
sentence length and newspapers
    63-64
shortening sentences 61-70
space 110, 112-113
speech marks 11, 25, 26
spelling 8
split infinitives 6, 11

standard letters 40, 88-93
stock phrases 35, 40, 42-43
style 6, 11, 16, 47, 54, 63, 93,
    95-106, 108, 128-129

target audience 3, 63, 111
tenses 13
typefaces 110-111

verbs 13, 45, 47